the scented home

living with fragrance

THIS IS A CARLTON BOOK

Design copyright © 2000 Carlton Books Limited
Text copyright © 2000 Karen Wheeler
This edition was published by Carlton Books Limited in 2000
20 Mortimer Street
London W1N 7RD

A CIP catalogue for this book is available from the British Library

ISBN 1 84222 049 7

Editorial Manager: **Venetia Penfold**

Art Director: **Penny Stock**

Project Editor: **Zia Mattocks**

Copy Editor: **Sarah Sears**

Photographer: **Polly Wreford**

Stylist: **Rose Hammick**

Production Manager: **Garry Lewis**

Printed and bound in Dubai

The author and publisher have made every effort to ensure that all
information on the use of essential oils is correct and up to date at
the time of publication. However, the application and quality of essential
oils is beyond the control of the above parties, who cannot be held
responsible for any problems resulting from their use.

Do not use essential oils without prior consultation with a qualified
aromatherapist if you are pregnant, taking any form of medication, or
if you suffer from oversensitive skin. Half-doses should be used for
children and the elderly.

the scented home

living with fragrance

karen wheeler

CARLTON
BOOKS

contents

introduction

Why bother to scent your home? The most obvious answer is that the aroma that permeates your living space – whether it is fresh grapefruit, sensual rose or stale cigarette smoke – says a great deal about you. In a world of designer products created to make our surroundings smell more pleasant, to be chic it is no longer enough to have the visual and touchy-feely trappings of good taste – the natural floors, subtle lighting and textured furnishings – it is equally necessary to have considered the olfactory experience, too.

Aromas can help to create a variety of moods and deliciously scented surroundings make us feel better. Recent research has shown that different aromas can soothe jangled nerves, promote sleep, boost the morale and help us to learn and work more effectively. Certain fragrances even act like drugs. The aroma of green apples, for example, can significantly reduce the severity of headaches and migraines; while green apples and cucumber can reduce claustrophobia.

Fragrance is a powerful form of therapy and one of the most effective ways to boost our sense of wellbeing. Through scent you can transform your home into a natural healing centre – a pleasurable and harmonious space in which to indulge the senses. Urban dwellers especially face a daily onslaught of pollution and unpleasant city smells. By perfuming your home you can not only take control of your environment, you can help to compensate for the poor air quality.

Fragrance can transport you to a better place and make daily living more pleasurable. It is also about savouring life – recreating the feeling you get when sitting in the garden on a warm summer evening with a chilled glass of Chablis, for example. Even reading or watching television can become sensual experiences when the room is dotted with flickering candles gently releasing perfume. How luxurious it is to slip between crisp, scented sheets when you go to bed. And if you can't go for a walk in a pine forest or by the sea, why not vaporize essential oils to evoke feelings of calm?

Our sense of smell is the key to unlocking a better mood or mind state – and it works more quickly than any drug. It takes just two seconds for an aroma to link up with the sensory receptors just behind the bridge of the nose and then travel to the area of the brain that governs emotions and memories. Aromachology, the research into the therapeutic qualities of scent, has shown that calming perfumes can have noticeable benefits in certain situations. When vanilla was vaporized at a cancer clinic in New York, patients reported a drop in their anxiety by as much as 65 per cent; scientists at Yale University have found that the smell of apple spice has an uncanny calming effect on people.

For all kinds of reasons – from pleasing the gods to warding off plague and disguising the smells of open sewers – people have scented their homes and surroundings since ancient times. One of the first reported uses of fragrance was the burning of incense or aromatic woods to ward off evil spirits and placate angry gods. In ancient Egypt dancing slaves wore scented cones on their heads and, as they moved, the cones melted and dispersed perfume into the air around them. Roman emperors poured rose-water into the canals running through their gardens. Denied access to the exotic smells of the Orient, Europeans relied on aromatic herbs, such as rosemary, thyme and lavender, which they scattered on floors to scent their homes and deter insects. By the sixteenth century recipes for fragranced waters and infused oils were widely available, and lavender bags and pomanders to perfume the home were commonplace. By this time spices were being brought back from the Orient, and the Elizabethans embraced them enthusiastically as a means of fragrancing both themselves and their homes. During the seventeenth century it was fashionable to drench every inch of the body, every article of clothing and every room in the house with a different perfume.

Nowadays we use scent in our living space more discerningly. It is no longer just a matter of disguising unpleasant odours; perfuming our surroundings has become an art – like flower arranging or interior decorating. And just as we choose colours and textures to suit individual rooms – lime green, for example, may be perfect for the kitchen but we wouldn't dream of using it all over our home – it makes sense to work with a selection of fragrances, using them to emphasize the mood of different rooms for different occasions. You can even have a venue scented professionally – Jo Malone once perfumed London's Royal Albert Hall with essential oils of jasmine, lime and rose for a fashion party.

The Scented Home takes you through the home room by room and looks at some of the ways in which you can use fragrance to enhance your environment and imprint it with your personality. With so many home-scent products created by international fragrance designers, such as Jo Malone, Diptyque, L'Artisan Parfumeur and Crabtree & Evelyn, we are spoilt for choice. There are delicate linen sprays, designer candles and incense, and super-chic sprays

'The scent you choose for your home is as important as the fine fragrance you wear on your skin.'

Jo Malone, perfumer

that look like expensive bottles of perfume. Home fragrance has certainly moved on from the synthetic air fresheners of old.

Any fragrance works most successfully when décor and scent are in harmony; when they are, the results can be quite magical. At the famous Farmaceutica di Santa Maria Novella in Florence, one of the oldest perfume houses in the world, the medicinal aromas of the herbal preparations still have a synergy with the timeless domes and frescoes. The pungent aromas transport you back to the thirteenth century, when the Dominican monks were cultivating herbs in their garden to prepare the balms, medications and creams for the monastery's infirmary. Similarly, at the very fashionable Hôtel Costes in Paris, the voluptuous smell of Turkish rose which permeates the rooms and corridors is perfectly in keeping with the swag curtains, red velvet chairs and sensuous lighting. It all adds up to an unforgettable and wickedly decadent atmosphere, not unlike a Turkish harem.

Dr Alan Hirsch of the Smell and Taste Treatment and Research foundation in Chicago has predicted that many homes in the future will use aroma-air-conditioning systems. These will pump out invigorating aromas to get you out of bed in the morning and relaxing scents when you return in the evening. It is likely that fragrance will be harnessed increasingly to technology. In Japan, for example, Shiseido has already joined forces with Seiko to produce an alarm clock that emits a blend of citrus, eucalyptus and pine to wake up your senses before the bell goes off. Scent is likely

to be used in more public places, too. Fragrance specialists Quest International have already developed a perfume for the Paris Metro; while a mixture of lemon and lavender could soon be used in airline cabins to help keep passengers calm.

In the future we can also expect more olfactorily enhanced home products. Scents are already being used in upholstery fabrics so that sofas will release fragrance when the cushions are plumped. And there is also a range of paints for children's bedrooms that incorporate 14 different smells, including bubble gum, chocolate biscuit and strawberry jam.

Experts are also predicting another big trend in the future: scenting your living space rather than yourself. There has already been a significant shift in emphasis, with Jo Malone's range of 'Living Colognes' – fragrances that you use on you skin *and* in your home so as to avoid clashing aromas. It all fits perfectly with the advice given by Stella Maris, a journalist in the 1930s, who recommended that women should stay faithful to a single perfume and use it not only to scent their skin and clothes but other personal effects, such as writing paper, cushions, books and bed, 'so that one single fragrance emanates from a person and everything they possess'.

For most of us, the choice is now too tantalizing to confine ourselves to just one fragrance. But one thing is for sure: burning a scented candle or spritzing the sheets with lavender spray has become as natural as squirting perfume on your pulse points. The future will indeed be fragrant.

the
1 essence
of home fragrance

The raw materials of fragrance are the fruit, petals, leaves and wood of a plant – be that a spice, herb or fruit. The essential oils extracted from these ingredients are in themselves an excellent source of home fragrance when vaporized; or they can be used to scent candles, bath oils, potpourris or incense sticks. Many flower and plant aromas are manufactured synthetically today, but the harsh scents of modern chemistry cannot and do not compare with nature's rich, aromatic treasures. Essential oils are extracted by various methods from different parts of the plant: lavender oil, for example, is obtained from the flowers, while ginger is extracted from the root and eucalyptus oil from the leaves. The ancient Chinese believed that they were liberating the soul of a plant when they extracted its oil.

making scents:
extracting precious oils

distillation

The method most often employed to extract essential oils from plants is distillation – a process that is thought to date back to tenth-century Persia. Either the petals, twigs, leaves or berries are placed in water, which is then brought to the boil – a process known as direct distillation; or the plant material is placed on a grill and the water heated underneath – steam distillation. The heat or steam breaks down the walls of the plant cells in which the essence is stored and the steam absorbs the essential oil. It is then cooled so that the water and oil separate.

enfleurage

Ironically, the most fragrant flowers, such as jasmine, rose and orange blossom, are the most difficult from which to extract fragrance. The intense heat involved in distillation would completely destroy the precious essences. Instead, a costly and time-consuming technique called enfleurage is used. The freshly picked petals are sprinkled over sheets of glass covered in animal fat, which absorbs the fragrance it draws from the petals. This process can take as long as three weeks, for when the petals fade, they are repeatedly replaced with fresh ones until the fat is saturated and can absorb no more essential oil. The oil–fat mixture is known as a pomade. The next stage involves washing the pomade with alcohol to obtain the extracts or 'absolutes'.

Absolutes contain more components of the plant from which they originate than essential oils obtained through distillation; because the scent is more concentrated, the aroma is fuller and more three-dimensional. Tuberose, jasmine, hyacinth and narcissus are all absolutes. Thus, the species that bear the least oil are the most expensive. It takes 100 kg (220 lb) of rose petals, for example, to produce a mere 50–80 ml (1½–2½ fl oz) of rose absolute.

solvent extraction

This is a very powerful method of extraction which makes it possible to obtain essences from tree bark or roots, or other plant parts that have only a faint aroma. The raw material is laid on perforated trays in extractors, and then a solvent is poured over it; this draws off the aromatic molecules as it runs though. The solvent is then filtered to remove the essential oil.

expression

This simple pressure technique is used to extract the oils from citrus fruits. The essential oils of lemon, lime, orange or bergamot are found in the outer, coloured layer of the rind of the fruit. When this is pressed, it ruptures the small pockets containing the essential oils. Although this is a straightforward method, it still takes 3,000 lemons to produce 1 kg (2¼ lb) of essential oil. Moreover, although there are machine methods, the best-quality citrus oils are still those extracted by hand.

the aroma groups

The scents used in home fragrance may be divided into several groups. Each of the different aroma groups has its own set of characteristics and lends itself well to a particular area of the home. As a general rule, the aromas extracted from the leaves or seeds of plants are good for rooms where a clean, fresh smell is required. The scent of eucalyptus, for example, is often found in kitchens and bathrooms – to create an atmosphere that suggests cleanliness. You would not, on the other hand – unless you were suffering in bed with 'flu – use eucalyptus in the bedroom. To some extent, we are conditioned to associate particular smells with certain activities or rooms. Lemon, for example, is linked in our psyches with cleanliness and kitchens. Despite its invigorating properties, we do not associate it with romance or sex. Instead, the scents most synonymous with the bedroom are the sweet, heady florals.

camomile
carnation
hyacinth
jasmine
lavender
linden blossom
mimosa
narcissus
neroli
rose maroc
rose otto
tuberose
ylang ylang

florals

Key rooms: bedroom and living room

The seductive powers of sweet, floral perfumes are put to best use in the bedroom, although they are equally popular for scenting living areas. Floral scents are traditionally associated with femininity and romance (Aphrodite, the Greek goddess of love, was said to be adorned with the blossoms of roses, narcissus, violets, hyacinths and lilies). Yet floral aromas used in the home are considered pleasant by both men and women, provided that they are not used to excess (the essential oils or absolutes are very concentrated so they should be used very sparingly). Rose is thought to be a particularly intoxicating fragrance, and is often a key ingredient in potpourri. Jasmine – perhaps because the flowers open and release their scent at night – is known as an aphrodisiac, as are the headier scents, such as narcissus, neroli and hyacinth. In the bedroom these fragrances are best used either as vaporized essential oils, or in scented candles or sprays. Do not feel obliged to confine the aromas of lavender and camomile to the bedroom, however, for they can create a relaxed mood in any room of the home.

herbs: basil
clary sage
marjoram
peppermint
oregano
rosemary
sage
thyme

herbaceous plants:
bay
cypress
eucalyptus
patchouli
petitgrain
tea tree

herbs &
herbaceous plants

Key rooms: study and kitchen

Fresh, green herbal aromas have a stimulating effect on the brain and can aid concentration. They are therefore ideal for work areas. The best way to take advantage of herbal scents in the study is to burn essential oils, but herbs can be used to scent the home in many inventive ways. You can tie a bunch of herbs under running bath water, for example; or add sprigs of sage, rosemary or lemon verbena to the glowing embers of a fire to fill the sitting room with their aromatic fragrance. The clean, sharp smell of growing herbs is also a good way to keep the air in the kitchen smelling fresh.

In Elizabethan times it was commonplace to strew strong-smelling herbs, such as rosemary and thyme, on floors. These released their aroma when walked on and not only disguised the unpleasant, everyday smells of unplumbed houses but also helped to repel insects and were believed to combat plague and disease, too. Our predecessors were probably unaware of the scientific foundation of their discovery but recent research has proven that certain herbs do indeed possess powerful antiviral and disinfectant properties.

grapefruit
lemon
lime
mandarin
orange
tangerine
juniper
bergamot

citrus & fruit

Key rooms: bathroom and kitchen

Citrus-fruit fragrances, such as grapefruit and lime, are perfect for the bathroom because they are sharp and invigorating. Lime, for example, is said to add laughter and playfulness (no bad thing on a gloomy winter morning). Lemon is usually associated with the kitchen and is one of the most popular fragrances for washing-up liquids, cleansers and room deodorizers. Most shower gels and household products featuring a citrus smell are artificially perfumed, but essential oils are preferable for scenting the home, as not only do they smell truly zesty but they also have natural cleansing and antiseptic properties. Citrus scents are rarely used in the bedroom, however – with the interesting exception of orange, which has calming, relaxing properties. Citrus scents are not renowned for possessing aphrodisiac qualities, although neroli oil (the essential oil of orange blossom) has a long-standing reputation as a sensuous scent.

Other fruit scents are popular for home fragrance – raspberry and peach, for example, are often used in scented candles and potpourris – but all too often they smell synthetic and sickly sweet. The advantages of citrus-fruit fragrance is that, even when it is synthetic rather than natural, it is not cloying. Moreover, as a general rule, the citrus fragrances as a group mix well with other fragrance categories: woody or herbal aromas, for example. One of the best examples is Jo Malone's bestselling lime, basil and mandarin bath oil, which has a fresh, sparkling, but sophisticated green smell.

cinnamon
clove
coriander
ginger
nutmeg
turmeric
black pepper

spices

Key rooms: kitchen and bedroom

Mysterious, warm and sexy in character, the spice aromas often feature prominently in scented products for the home. Ginger, clove and cinnamon, for example, are all popular ingredients in potpourri and scented candles. Because they help to create a warm ambience, spicy scents come into their own during the winter months. Similar in aroma to mulled wine and plum pudding, they are now particularly associated with Christmas. Certainly, they are ideal for creating a cosy atmosphere in the kitchen and for disguising cooking smells. And because they are thought to 'spice up' love lives, spicy smells are also used in the bedroom.

As an alternative to burning essential oils from the spice family, you can also vaporize whole spices in the hot water of an oil burner; you should allow 30 minutes for the scent to permeate the room. Try using vanilla pods, cloves, ginger root, grated nutmeg or cinnamon bark, either singly or in combination. Also bear in mind that spicy aromas combine well with sweet smells: cinnamon and orange, for example, is a popular mix, and a crushed cinnamon stick really combines well with dried rose petals in potpourri.

Historically, spicy scents were used to mask the smell of decay – whether of decomposing food or bodies. The Egyptians relied heavily on spices such as cinnamon for embalming the dead, and physicians in the Middle Ages wore clothes impregnated with the smell of cloves, cinnamon and other spices as a form of protection when they were treating plague victims.

cedarwood
pine woods
rosewood
sandalwood

Key rooms: sitting room and bedroom

The essential oils extracted from the twigs, bark or wood chippings of trees are considered very masculine and earthy, and yet sensuous. Cedarwood, for example, because it contains a high concentration of essential oil, is very aromatic. However, it is difficult to unleash the essential oils from some woody plants and trees as the essence is stored in ducts in the fibrous part of the wood or bark; the woody material has to be crushed or broken down before the oil is extracted. Nevertheless, aromatic woods have been burned or used for incense since ancient times, when the rich, strong scents were offered to the gods as gifts. In China, peasants still place piles of smouldering plants and sticks under their beds – not only for warmth but also to infuse their homes with a rich, woody aroma.

This family of fragrances works particularly well in the living room. You can either burn the essential oils or incense sticks; or, if you have a log fire, try adding a few drops of essential oil of pine, sandalwood, cypress or cedarwood to each log, about 30 minutes before you plan to use it. This should give the oil time to seep into the wood and scent it. Pine essential oil is also excellent for banishing the smell of cigarette smoke: simply add 10 drops to 150 ml (5 fl oz) of water to make up a room spray. Woody scents combine well with spicy aromas and create a warm, welcoming ambience in the sitting room.

benzoin frankincense myrrh amber

resins

Key rooms: hallway and study

The highly aromatic scents of frankincense, myrrh, amber and benzoin are mysterious and soothing in character. Because they smell dark and musky rather than fresh and clean, you would not use these fragrances in kitchens, but rather to evoke an atmosphere or mood in other rooms of the home. What better way to create a warm, welcoming atmosphere in an entrance hall than with the exotic oils of the gum-yielding trees of the Orient? They work especially well with Oriental-style décor or dark wood interiors; and are also well suited to libraries and studies.

Frankincense, a sweet-smelling, reddish-brown resin from North Africa and Arabia is a truly beautiful essential oil, said to lift the spirits and cure depression. One of the most highly prized and valuable substances of the ancient world, it was often used to banish evil spirits. Today it is often associated with Christmas and closely linked with myrrh – a smoky, bitter-smelling resin, produced by a tree which grows in Libya, Iran and northeast Africa. Benzoin is another dark reddish-brown resin but it is derived from a tree which grows in Thailand. It smells of vanilla and, like myrrh and frankincense, it has very warming, soothing qualities. Resin fragrances usually combine well with rose.

2 live

a fragrant match

Smell plays an important role in how we react to our environment. Studies in the USA have shown that people will linger for longer in a pleasant-smelling atmosphere. So if you want to make your guests feel at ease, the living areas of your home should be fragranced in such a way as to evoke warm, welcoming feelings. Lavender or geranium oils are ideal for this purpose.

There are other factors to take into account when scenting your living space. Ideally, you should match a fragrance with the surroundings. Sweet floral smells work with chintz décor and cosy country cottages, but in loft spaces and more modern environments, old-fashioned rose potpourri seems out of place and clean, citrus smells work better. Moreover, just as perfumes react and smell differently on different people, so it is with fragrance and living spaces. Buildings have their own intrinsic smell. A Swiss ski chalet, for example, has a very different odour to a New York apartment. Similarly, a room containing leather furniture, old books and a wood fire will have little in common scent-wise with a centrally heated room furnished with cotton drill sofas and a glass table. So try to choose a fragrance that complements the natural aroma of your home. Generally speaking, warmer, spicier smells (such as amber, vanilla, sandalwood or myrrh) work well in wood- and leather-rich environments, while refreshing scents (such as green tea or citrus) suit rooms where there is a lot of chrome and glass.

a scent for all seasons (and all reasons)

Unlike other elements of interior design, fragrance can be changed to suit the season. Try vaporizing oils with cooling properties, like peppermint, cucumber, coriander or lime, in the heat of the summer. In the winter rosewood, cinnamon, black pepper, ginger and sandalwood are among the oils that will help to create a warm, cosy atmosphere.

Similarly, you can alter the scent of a room to enhance your mood. Try lavender or camomile if you want to chill out after a hard day; jasmine or rose if you feel emotionally drained or low; bergamot or an invigorating mixture of lemon and lime if you need to be revitalized.

'Choosing an environmental **fragrance** is like creating an olfactory **décor**.'

Jean-Françoise Laporte, perfumer

'The scent of **rose** with a base of woody notes and a hint of oriental **spice** is **warm** and welcoming and one of my favourite wintry, **fireside** smells.'

Nina Campbell, interior designer

banishing bad odours

To abolish unwanted smells – such as eau de dog or old trainers – make a room spray, which can also be spritzed onto carpets and soft furnishings, by adding a few drops of lemongrass or bergamot oil to water. This will remove stale odours and is better than a canned spray because these essential oils have antiseptic and antibacterial qualities. To mask the smell of stale tobacco smoke, try using a woody scent such as patchouli, pine or cedarwood. If you do not like woody aromas, try saturating cotton wool in grapefruit oil and placing it behind a radiator or in the hem of the curtains.

beating the bugs

Fragrance can also be employed to help to combat germs and viruses. If somebody in your household has had 'flu, for example, there are several essential oils which can be used to prevent the infection from spreading. Tea tree, eucalyptus and pine are not only bracing fragrances but also have an antiseptic effect. Simply make a spray by diluting 10–20 drops in 100 ml (3½ fl oz) of water and spritz it into the air. Tea tree is fairly pungent so you may not be able to bear the smell. You might try making an environmental fragrance instead by blending 2 drops of bergamot, 3 drops of lemon, 2 drops of geranium, 5 drops of clary sage and 1 drop of basil or rosemary in 100 ml (3½ fl oz) of water. Shake vigorously and spray the air around you.

The fresh leaves of fragrant herbs such as thyme, rosemary, hyssop and sage contain natural antiseptics and have been used to improve hygiene for hundreds of years. Rosemary or juniper sprigs continued to be burnt in French hospitals until relatively recently to help purify the air. If you have an open fire, you can add sprigs of fresh herbs to it, but in most modern homes it is easier to use the essential oils – either in sprays or in a burner or light-bulb ring. (Juniper, tea tree or pine oils also make excellent household disinfectants – use a few drops in 500 ml (17 fl oz) of water to wash floors and other surfaces.)

introducing fragrance

There are many different and effective ways to perfume a room, and these all vary considerably in potency and durability. In addition to choosing a fragrance, take into account the kind of atmosphere you want to create – a quick, refreshing spritz with a citrus room spray, for example, will create a completely different ambience from that of a soothing scented candle or warming spicy incense.

holy smoke: incense sticks

The perfume of incense is perhaps most often associated with religious ceremonies. Ever since ancient times, and still today, the aromatic scents of burning woods have been used to suffuse sacred places with pleasant aromas. In Buddhist monasteries in Tibet, incense is still used to heighten the senses and stimulate meditation. In India, meanwhile, holy places are often suffused with the smell of sandalwood.

Religious purposes aside, incense is perhaps most often associated – at least in the West – with teenagers attempting to disguise the smell of cigarette smoke in their bedrooms. Although incense has suffered from its leftover hippie image, it is rapidly becoming one of the most fashionable and sophisticated ways to scent the home, and it is often more subtle and less cloying than candles. Many incense sticks or cones are sold with a special holder or dish. Alternatively, you can anchor them in a little container of sand or rock salt. Blow out the flame immediately after lighting, and allow the aromatic stick to smoulder gently, releasing its fragrant smoke in the process. This gradually fades away, leaving a subtle fragrance that lasts for 30 minutes to an hour.

cut flowers and plants

No synthetic fragrance can compete with the smell of fresh flowers and people have always sought to capture this in the home. In the nineteenth century violets were grown in lidded glass jars, which kept the air around the flowers humid so that a heady waft of fragrance

was released when the lid was lifted. Another nineteenth-century practice – which makes a stylish and fragrant table decoration – was to float flower heads in a bowl of water.

Sales of fresh cut flowers have rocketed in recent times. Whereas they were once only bought for special occasions, flowers are now seen as an important home accessory and bought on a regular basis. But buying and choosing flowers has become something of a style minefield – almost as subject to fashion trends as heel heights and hemlines. Orchids, for example, have recently been the victim of stem snobbery: hugely desirable one minute, only to be declared passé the next. There are certain fragrant flowers, however, which enjoy classic status and are always popular. Roses, hyacinths and lilies are some of the best stems for scenting a room; in the spring, a simple glass vase filled with fragrant freesias is a visual and olfactory pleasure. The key is to have one type of flower and to have lots of it. If your favourite bloom is unperfumed, you can always mix it with aromatic foliage such as eucalyptus.

House plants can also bring colour and perfume to your home and they help to purify the air, too. Hyacinths are easy to grow and are one of the sweetest-smelling flowering plants. Scented geraniums, much in demand during the reign of Charles I for scenting musty rooms, also grow well indoors, as they require minimal maintenance – only a little water throughout the year. (They are particularly suitable for town flats where there is restricted natural light.) Other plants such as areca palms, spider plants and bamboo palms actually extract toxic substances from the air. They are also believed to absorb some of the harmful emissions that are the product of computer technology.

Some trend predictors believe that in the future urban dwellers with no access to a garden will devote a space or even a room in their home to live greenery, in order to feel in touch with nature. Even now you could cultivate a window box: the scent of flowers or herbs wafting in through the window of a town flat on a summer's day can be very uplifting. Many herbs grow well in such a confined space, including basil, cotton lavender, rosemary, thyme and golden marjoram. They can also be grown in tubs indoors – along with clary sage and lemon verbena. This has an added advantage in that certain herbs, such as basil, also repel insects and flies. As an extra deterrent, try rubbing the leaves on window frames or in problem areas.

'Scented **candles** are a simple way to bring **fragrance** into any environment and add instant **ambience**.'

Jo Malone, perfumer

candles

Whether in the form of dozens of tiny tea-lights clustered around a room or one huge sculptural block of wax, scented candles are the most popular way to infuse a room with fragrance and create the right atmosphere. One of the first fragranced candles in the UK – believed to be scented with blueberry – was created in 1893 by Prices, the royal warrant holder. Rigaud, the French perfume house famous for its scented candles, created its first fragrant candle as late as 1950, despite a history in scent dating back to the early nineteenth century. However, it was in the late 1980s that scented candles really captured the imagination when – along with wooden floors and white walls – they became a symbol of stylish living. In the decade when many people had money to burn, they did so literally, in the form of expensive slabs of designer wax. Fashion designer Donna Karan once threw a memorable party in London, lit entirely by great banks of white candles. Nowadays, the trend seems to be for oversized blocks of wax – ideally, sculpted into interesting shapes. Anne Severine Liotard's floor-standing candles, for example, are almost works of art and could easily form the centrepiece for a room.

Although there are many different types of candle available, it is worth paying extra for a top make, such as Diptyque or Rigaud. Not only is the fragrance of a better quality (some cheap brands smell horribly synthetic); expensive candles generally burn more slowly and contain more fragrance. A Rigaud candle, for example, contains the equivalent amount of fragrance as a 50 ml (1½ fl oz) eau-de-toilette spray. The type of wax is vital: soft wax not only holds more perfume, but diffuses it more effectively, scenting the room better than harder waxes. The softness also allows the candle to burn uniformly, so that the candle retains its shape and remains flat and even on top. Soft wax candles often come in their own glass pots or decorative containers. It is also possible to make your own scented candles – by vaporizing essential oils in molten candle wax. If you extinguish the flame, add a few drops of oil and re-light the candle, it should release the fragrance for up to two hours.

'Candles can be **beautiful** sculptures but they are **practical** and useful in bringing a space **alive**.'

Anne Severine Liotard, candle sculptress

A very stylish way to incorporate candles in a room is to float small, flat candles in a bowl of water. A cluster of chubby candles placed in a fake fireplace makes a good substitute for a real fire and helps to give a room a focal point as well as a cosy ambience. In addition to general living areas, candles work well dotted around the side of the bathtub or on your bedside table. For outdoor use, choose candles containing citronella. This helps to repel mosquitoes – worth remembering in hotter climates.

vaporizing oils

Essential oils are extremely volatile and release their fragrance most effectively when in contact with heat. You can burn oils in several ways. Oil burners, made from porcelain or pottery, are very popular. They comprise a dish for water, into which you sprinkle a few drops of essential oil, which is then heated by a night-light in a lower compartment; the oil-and-water mixture is thus vaporized, releasing fragrance into the air. Using an electric diffuser is safer because there is no water or naked flame involved – ideal for an office. You simply drop the oil neat onto a porcelain stone, which is then heated electronically. You can also vaporize oils on special rings which fit around light bulbs. As the bulb heats up, the fragrant vapours are released. Diffusing essential oils like this is one of the best ways to create a mood – invigorating, calming or relaxing – and to provide a room with continuous fragrance. Some of the most popular oils for burning are lavender, bergamot and geranium.

cut and dried: potpourri

The name for this fragrant and decorative mix of perfumed petals, leaves, stems, spices and flower heads comes from the French; it actually means 'rotten pot'. There are all kinds of potpourri recipes for different occasions and rooms in the house, many dating back to the eighteenth century, when their purpose was simply to mask the stench of everyday life. Potpourri was originally used only in the houses of the aristocracy; it consisted of bowls of fresh petals and aromatic wood shavings, which were then sprinkled with salt in order to preserve the colour and fragrance – a far cry from the mass-produced bags of artificially fragranced and coloured wood shavings which are often sold today as potpourri.

Potpourri's image has undoubtedly suffered because of this poor imitation. There is a trend among top fragrance houses, however, to update the concept, using more interesting- and contemporary-looking ingredients, such as big seed pods and scrunched-up pieces of citrus fruit. It is the texture and shape of the ingredients that determines how modern and appealing it looks.

It can be very satisfying to make your own potpourri. If you do not wish to display it in bowls left on a shelf to gather dust, you can use potpourri in clothes sachets, scatter cushions, in curtain hems or anywhere else where heat, contact or movement will release the scent. The one real disadvantage of potpourri is that it needs to be revived regularly (at least every two months) using perfumed oil.

Rose petals and lavender are the two basic ingredients in classical potpourri as they retain their perfume well. Other fashionable flowers to use include lime blossom, heliotrope, hyacinth, lilac, lily-of-the-valley, violet and orange blossom. It is vital to harvest flowers, leaves, berries and roots at the correct time. Flowers, for example, must be gathered when the blooms are on the point of opening or have only just opened, so as to conserve the essential oils which would otherwise be given off as perfume. Thus, you should avoid cut flowers that have been picked for some time and blooms that have already opened; they will already have started to fade and lose their scent, and the edges of the petals will simply curl and go brown. When you are selecting your ingredients, flowers should dominate the mixture. Use smaller quantities of scented leaves because that fragrance tends to be stronger: the best recipes combine 1 part of dried aromatic leaves with 7 parts of flower petals. Use spices sparingly, too, in a ratio of about 1 tablespoon to 4 cups of flowers and leaves.

Practically any object, including pebbles and stones, can be impregnated with fragrance. Conifer cones or pieces of bark will add texture and visual interest to a potpourri mix, and chunks or slices of citrus fruit are both fragrant and decorative additions. You should soak the cones in a mixture of water and pine oil to enhance their natural fragrance, and simply cut thin slices of lime, lemon or orange and either air- or oven-dry them.

'Huge Chinese **bowls** full of **potpourri** and placed on the floor can look **magnificent** in a room with sunlight pouring through.'

Nicky Haslam, interior designer

The really essential ingredient is a fixative, which prolongs the life of potpourri by capturing and retaining some of the fragrance molecules. Orrisroot (*Iris florentina*) is the most readily available and does not influence the blend too strongly. Use one tablespoon per two to four cups of potpourri mixture.

Once you have selected your ingredients, lay them out for a few days to dry – ideally on old net curtains, but otherwise on newspaper or muslin – in a dry place but not in direct sunlight. Then stir them together with fixatives and essential oils and store the mixture in an airtight container in a dry, dark, warm place for approximately six weeks, shaking it gently from time to time. Depending on the ingredients, the total drying process can take anything from five days to two months, but the scent and colour are retained better when a slow method is used. Crush some ingredients but leave others to be broken up later to prolong the life of the potpourri. To release the scent effectively, turn the mixture regularly and refresh the fragrance with a few drops of essential oil derived from the dominant flower or fruit in your mix.

pomanders

Elizabethans loved spices and essences brought back from the Orient. They wore them around their neck or hanging from their waist, in pomanders made of carved silver spheres in order to mask unpleasant odours (often their own) and surround themselves with fragrance. Nowadays, we are more likely to hang simple clove-studded orange pomanders in our wardrobes where they can be used to deter moths, or as festive decorations, hung on bright ribbons around the house or on the Christmas tree, filling the air with their delicious scent. In China oranges are a symbol of wealth and happiness and are used as a gift during the Chinese New Year. Orange is the ultimate sunny and happy fragrance, whose aroma is said to balance the nervous system and banish negative emotions. It blends well with spicy aromas other than clove, such as cinnamon, for instance. It is a wonderful fragrance for winter, thanks to its warm, rounded and cheering aroma.

orange and clove pomanders

Oranges take at least a year to dry out, so make them at Christmas time and they will be ready for the following year. Use thin-skinned oranges and pierce holes in the skin with a cocktail stick, either all over or in a vertical stripe pattern, then push the cloves into the holes. Wrap each orange individually in a brown paper bag and put them in a dark, warm place, such as an airing cupboard, and leave them to dry out slowly (don't put them anywhere too warm as they will turn mouldy). Once the oranges have dried out, then dust them with orrisroot powder which acts as a fixative, prolonging the life and fragrance. Attach ribbons and hang them around the house.

spray perfumes

The fastest way to banish an unpleasant odour is with a perfumed spray. The new generation of home fragrance sprays come in elegant glass flaçons that are much more sophisticated than aerosol cans. Some of them smell so good that you could actually be tempted to spritz them on your pulse points – which is, in fact, the very idea. Top fragrance houses are now producing spray scents which can be used on your skin as well as on sheets, carpets and towels. This is likely to be a key trend for fragrance in the future, as it makes sense to avoid clashing fragrances and to combine your personal scent with that of your home. If you prefer naturally fragranced sprays, you can make you own by adding 5 drops of your favourite essential oil to 150 ml (5 fl oz) of warm water in a clean plant mister. Shake the mixture vigorously, then spritz it into the atmosphere. A spray containing 20 drops of eucalyptus, tea tree or bergamot oil and 200 ml (7 fl oz) of water is an excellent way to disinfect a room.

soft touch: perfumed linen and furnishings

What could be more sensuous than scented linen and soft furnishings? This is one of the most subtle and refined ways to fragrance the home as you have to be up close to experience it. Aromatic scatter cushions are a good way of perfuming living areas because they will release their scent when leant against. If you do not have the time to sew your own (and who does?), simply slip a sachet filled with lavender or other dried flowers inside a pillowcase or cushion cover. Luxurious fabrics such as silk, fur, cashmere and pashmina hold fragrance really well. The ultimate home luxury is an old pashmina shawl, cashmere blanket or cushion sprayed with your favourite scent and draped over your bed or a chair.

Louis XIV employed an army of servants whose sole duty was to boil his shirts in nutmeg, cloves, jasmine, orange blossom and musk. You can perfume your clothes by putting sachets of lavender or other dried flowers in cupboards and drawers. To scent linen naturally, add a solution of a clear essential oil, such as lavender, pine, lemon or rosewood (so as not to stain the clothing), to the final rinse in the washing machine. Alternatively, put 5 drops of essential oil on a handkerchief and place it in the tumble dryer with your clothes, sheets or towels.

exotic

'A home **perfume** must suggest an **atmosphere** without ever invading it.'

Jean-Françoise Laporte, perfumer

3 eat

scent of an oven

Is it any wonder that when it is suffused with mouthwatering food smells, like the warm, comforting aromas of biscuits being baked, wine being mulled or casseroles simmering in the oven, a kitchen draws us in like bees to a honey pot? Often the soul of the home, it can provide a feast for the senses: delicious aromas, tantalizing tastes and visual delights. One of the most heavenly kitchen smells of all – sometimes used to entice buyers when a house is being sold – is the aroma of toast mingled with that of freshly brewed coffee. Scientists believe that food smells make people feel warm and cosy. They unlock positive childhood memories – watching your mother bake cakes in a warm kitchen, for example – reminding us of a time when life seemed happy and secure.

Delicious smells also play an important role in our appreciation of food as our sense of taste is in fact largely dependent on our sense of smell: 90 per cent of 'taste' or 'flavour' is actually smell. Without it our tongues can distinguish only four flavours: sweet, sour, salty and bitter. Take away the sense of smell and it would be hard to differentiate between a savoury risotto and a sweet rice pudding. So, it is no coincidence that the words often used to describe smells, such as 'delicious', 'mouthwatering' or 'appetizing', also form an integral part of the vocabulary used to describe food.

Whereas messages from the other senses – sight, touch, taste and hearing – are edited during their journey to the brain, smell has a direct 'hotline', which is why the aroma of coffee has the capacity to lure us out of bed on a cold winter morning and kickstart a sluggish mind even before we have taken the first sip. The fact that people respond positively to food smells is something that supermarkets have been quick to exploit. Many of them now pump food smells through the aisles – freshly baked bread, rich, heady chocolate or the spicy aromas of cinnamon or Christmas pudding – in order to whet our appetite and tempt us to spend more.

'The **smell** of buttered toast simply talked to Toad ... of **warm** kitchens, of breakfasts on **bright** frosty mornings, of **cosy** parlour firesides ...'

Kenneth Grahame, *The Wind in the Willows*

fake it
... if you can't bake it

doing it without doing it
(cooking aromas, that is)

The most natural kitchen smells, of food cooking, are the best of all. But we live in an era where people are often too busy even to rinse a lettuce leaf much less prepare and cook a nourishing, balanced meal from scratch. Consequently, the only food aromas emanating from many kitchens come from last night's takeaway or the synthetic, plastic smell of pre-packed food being blasted in the microwave – somehow these are not quite as appealing as the smells of home-cooked food sizzling slowly in the oven.

For those who are too busy to boil an egg, let alone bake cakes, however, fashionable fragrance companies have cooked up room sprays that emulate a selection of truly mouthwatering food smells. A quick squirt and you can fill your kitchen with anything from the smell of fresh, newly rinsed salad greens to the rich aromas of a French patisserie – without so much as opening the fridge door. American company Demeter, for example, has bottled the smell of a wide range of foodstuffs including tomato, cinnamon toast, cappuccino, tiramisu and sugar cookie. The 'gin-and-tonic' room spray is even designed to give you a little fillip – just like the real thing. Demeter compares its fragrances to a virtual experience: doing it without doing it. In other words, if you do not have time to cook, spraying culinary aromas is the next best thing.

gourmet scents

The natural fragrances of herbs, spices and fruits have long been popular for scenting the home. But the most recent trend is for enticing dairy, bakery and sweet candy smells, which are even being featured in many beauty and fine fragrance products. In the USA, particularly, comforting and nostalgic food smells are currently huge favourites.

Several years ago perfumers started including food notes in scents. Thierry Mugler's Angel, a heady mix of chocolate and caramel, was considered particularly groundbreaking when it was launched in 1992. Now aromas such as chocolate, cinnamon, ginger and even green tea have become commonplace. Fragrance houses are constantly searching for more exotic ingredients – although, thankfully, none as yet has tried to incorporate the smell of onions or garlic.

home sweet home

The sweet smell of chocolate and cake-baking seems to have a particularly powerful effect on the psyche. Vanilla is a warm, sensuous fragrance that triggers memories of custard, ice cream and cakes; more physiologically direct and less evocative, the merest sniff of a slab of chocolate can make people as happy and euphoric as when they are eating it. The aroma of chocolate has even been shown to boost serotonin levels in the brain – an effect it shares with certain antidepressant drugs. This may explain the success of a company like Boston-based Fresh, for example, which began by making chocolate-scented soaps but quickly expanded their range to include Fleurs de Chocolat – four fragrances with dark chocolate notes – as well as chocolate-scented candles and incense sticks. Another sweet aroma that is currently popular in home fragrance is fig – a favourite of interior designer Nicky Haslam, who describes its scent as 'warm and voluptuous'.

vanilla

A member of the orchid family, vanilla has been an ingredient in fragrance and food ever since Aztec times, when it was used to flavour chocolate. The best vanilla essence comes from the island of Réunion in the Indian Ocean and is known as Bourbon vanilla. The green vanilla pods need to 'sweat' for several months under cover before they release their fragrance. The pods can be used in potpourri; the essential oil, meanwhile, when vaporized, releases an aroma which is warm, relaxing and sensuous.

'I poured a glass of **chocolate** for myself, with noisette liqueur and **hazelnut** chips. The **smell** is warm and intoxicating, like that of a woodpile in the late autumn **sun**.'

Joanne Harris, *Chocolat*

scenting and cleansing
with essential oils

Some fragrance experts believe that the kitchen should be a place of 'olfactory silence'; that it is one room where strong scents that could be overpowering to food should be avoided. But how do you set about eliminating unpleasant cooking odours? Rather than using chemical sprays and cleansers, choose natural essences to purify the air: synthetic deodorizers can often interact with the very smells that they are meant to be disguising and can actually make them worse. The kitchen is also the one room where you should try to avoid introducing toxic mixes of chemicals.

As a general rule, opt for essential oils or extracts of ingredients that you would be likely to find in the kitchen. Rosemary, juniper, sage, mint, orange, cinnamon and cucumber can all help to diffuse odours. Spicy aromas blend in particularly well in the kitchen and are good for disguising food smells, while citrus scents such as lemon and grapefruit are very cleansing and refreshing.

One of the best ways to combat overpowering cooking smells is to light a lemon verbena candle. The odour of festering rubbish can be pretty unpleasant, too, so to counteract it, try rinsing out the bin with a few drops of a citrus or tea-tree oil diluted in warm water every time you empty it. Tea tree, eucalyptus and pine oils not only have bracing aromas but also a strong antiseptic effect. To disinfect the kitchen, dilute 20 drops of tea tree oil in 100 ml (3½ fl oz) of water in a clean plant spray; shake the solution vigorously and then spray the air around you. If you do not like the strong smell of tea tree, use bergamot or another citrus oil. Alternatively, blend juniper – which has purifying and antiseptic effects – with a citrus oil.

tea tree oil

The tea tree (*Melaleuca alternifolia*) grows exclusively in northeast Australia. When the feathery, green leaves are distilled, a pale yellow oil with a pungent camphor-like smell results. Not everybody likes the aroma, but it acts powerfully against bacteria, fungi and viruses. Modern science first acknowledged tea tree's medicinal properties in 1930, when experiments revealed that it was 12 times stronger than carbolic acid, the standard antiseptic ingredient at the time.

delicious

handy herbs

Herbs are naturally at home in the kitchen. They smell wonderfully fresh and sharp and also help to deter insects. Rosemary and thyme also have antiseptic properties; for centuries, indeed, they were used to fumigate sick rooms.

Herbs can be used to create a visual as well as an aromatic feast for the senses. For a 'live' potpourri, try filling terracotta pots or other decorative containers with your favourite herbs: rosemary, thyme, basil and sage are ideal. Alternatively, make a herb garland (see opposite) and keep it next to the oven. Not only will it purify the air but it is very handy for cooking; you can just rip off leaves as and when you need them. Remember that it is better to tear the fresh leaves to release the warm, spicy flavour rather than cutting them.

how to make a culinary garland

Home stylist Claire Richardson has devised the perfect way to display herbs and scent the kitchen at the same time. Measure a piece of thin florist's wire the desired length of your garland, add an extra 15 cm (6 in) at each end to make the loops from which it will hang, and cut the wire. Thread a darning needle with the wire and wire up the following ingredients: dried oranges and orange slices (available from good florists or, alternatively, see page 48 for how to make your own), cinnamon sticks, fresh sprigs of rosemary, fresh or dry red chillies, and some fresh or dry bay leaves. To create an attractive and striking visual effect, wire up groups of ingredients along the length of the garland. Last of all, add some bouquet garni posies, using separate pieces of wire for each one to enable you to pull them off individually when you want to use them.

perfumed party tricks

The Roman emperor Nero is reported to have drowned his guests during banquets in a fragrant sea of rose petals. On other occasions he is said to have sprayed them with different oils to put them in the mood of his choice. All very well, but if you are entertaining friends at home you need a fragrance that will enhance the atmosphere without being overpowering and which will not clash with the smell of the food. A strong fragrance can even spoil the taste of a dish, which is why many restaurants have taken the step of banning some particularly potent perfumes. It is a good idea as well to avoid smells that have been proven to kill the appetite (see page 77). There are, however, many warming, larger-than-life aromas that will encourage lively company. While they cannot transform turgid bores into witty Oscar Wilde types, they will help to put people in sparkling good spirits. A few drops of geranium, melissa and cinnamon vaporized before your guests arrive will always help; cinnamon's spiciness, for example, is very energizing and invigorating. If you sprinkle clary sage oil around the room it will promote a lively, even euphoric, atmosphere; its pungent, warm, nutty aroma is said to have 'feel-good' properties, even producing a sensation of mild inebriation.

You can match the fragrance to the occasion, too. Rose and ylang ylang are perfect for a romantic dinner; pine, orange and frankincense combine well for a Christmas party; if the food is hot and spicy, sandalwood and patchouli are ideal.

'What a **wonderful**
pleasure it is to enter a room
that smells **delicious**.'

Nina Campbell, interior designer

fragrant table decorations

Although you can buy delicious ready-made potpourri suitable for the kitchen, you really should try making it yourself if you want the best results. A mixture of cloves, cinnamon sticks and dried oranges makes a wonderful kitchen potpourri in the winter. Moreover, as well as burning essential oils or fragrant candles, it is possible to introduce fragrance with scented table decorations and aromatic bundles of fresh herbs. Tying cinnamon sticks together with brightly coloured ribbons is a really easy way to decorate a winter dining table, for example. In the summer you can simply place a frangipani stem at each place setting. Alternatively, a wire frame entwined with ivy and fragrant flowers set around a short, wide candle makes a stylish table decoration. Simplest of all, you could follow the lead of interiors stylist Carolyn Quartermaine and scatter fresh rose petals – available in boxes from top florists – across the dining table.

cinnamon

There are many species of cinnamon but the variety that is used as a cooking spice is the dried inner bark of a tropical evergreen tree found in Madagascar, parts of Asia and southeast Africa. The essential oil is extracted from the bark or the leaf and is used as a minor ingredient in essential oil blends; it combines well with benzoin, cedarwood, orange and cypress. Like many of the spice aromas, cinnamon is considered warming and stimulating. It is good for entertaining as it helps to create a convivial atmosphere. It is also considered to be an aphrodisiac. To scent the kitchen, cinnamon sticks can be crushed into a potpourri or used on their own – tied in aromatic bundles or placed in a small vase or glass.

an appetite for scents

Certain aromas are said to stimulate the appetite as well as the brain. These include bergamot, lemongrass and coriander. Coriander is also believed to aid digestion and has been used in the treatment of anorexia nervosa. If on the other hand, you are trying to lose weight, the aroma of green apples is said to curb the appetite. Fennel, too, can be used to suppress hunger. In Roman times, soldiers on long marches carried fennel seeds to chew until their next meal, and in the Middle Ages Christians used fennel to help them get through days of fasting.

tips for the kitchen

• To clean the fridge or freezer: dilute a few drops of orange or grapefruit essential oil in 1 litre (1¾ pints) of warm water and use a clean cloth to wipe the inside of the appliance thoroughly.

• For an antiseptic surface cleaner, which is equally good for rinsing floors: add 5 drops of an antiseptic oil, such as tea tree or bergamot, to 1 litre (1¾ pints) of warm water.

• To freshen up the kitchen bin: sprinkle several drops of tea tree, lavender or lemon oil onto a damp cloth and use it to wipe out the inside of the bin.

• As a room freshener and fly deterrent: grow deliciously sweet-spicy basil in a pot or window box.

• It sounds unlikely, but striking a match will also help to eliminate cooking smells.

4 work

scents for the mind

Scent can play a significant role in focusing the mind and boosting efficiency. The crisp, green aromas of herbs such as rosemary, basil, thyme and coriander seem to have a particularly stimulating effect, although citrus scents have also been shown to bring noticeable benefits. Using essential oils is the best means of boosting mental performance. You can either scent your home office or study continuously by diffusing oils in a burner or take 'aromatic breaks', inhaling a few drops of an invigorating essential oil on a handkerchief.

Ever since Dr Shizuo Torii demonstrated that different essential oils can affect performance in different ways, office-fragrancing has been taken very seriously in Japan.

When a bank vaporized lemon essence in its offices over a period of a month, for example, input operators' errors were reduced by nearly 50 per cent. It is commonplace today for Japanese companies to diffuse lemon in their offices after lunch – to minimize mid-afternoon lethargy – and in business meetings, to increase mental alertness. Similar findings resulted from a study by the Fragrance Research Fund where half the control group were asked to proofread material in a non-fragranced room and the balance worked in a room scented with peppermint and lavender: the latter performed 'significantly better'.

how aromas stimulate the brain

People have been using plant essences for years to invigorate themselves and make themselves more alert. The chemical make-up of essential oils is very complex, however, and while we know that a certain aroma can stimulate the mind or effect a particular change of mood, we cannot explain scientifically exactly how it does so. As to why the aroma of lemon increases alertness, evidence suggests that limonene, one of the active ingredients in citrus oils (including grapefruit and bergamot) actually increases circulation, which in turn boosts oxygen flow to the brain. Similarly, the essential oils of the sage family, which includes thyme, rosemary and marjoram, contain thymol. This substance appears to boost alertness and modulate the nervous system but is currently the subject of scientific research, of particular interest because of its possible effects on Alzheimer's disease.

rosemary for remembering

The scent of rosemary is good for combating lethargy and for boosting confidence. The essential oil has a particularly piercing aroma and stimulates both the nervous system and the brain. It also has antiseptic qualities. Originating on the coasts of the Mediterranean, rosemary was one of the earliest plants to be used in medicine and fragrance: in ancient Greece country people who could not afford incense burnt sprigs of rosemary on their shrines. An attractive bush, with silver-green, needle-shaped leaves and pale blue flowers, rosemary now grows freely all over Europe.

memory enhancement

The sense of smell appears to be strongly linked to memory (think of how the smell of a perfume can transport you vividly back to the time and place when you wore it). We know that aroma molecules gain immediate access to our mind, mood and emotions through the olfactory bulb, which is housed just above the nose. And we also know that there is a direct link between the olfactory bulb and the limbic part of the brain, where memory, among other things, is controlled and contained. While we do not know exactly how they send memory-evoking signals to the brain, the aromas of ginger, basil, lemon, grapefruit, rosemary, coriander and peppermint are all thought to aid memory and powers of recall. A study carried out at Yale University in the USA demonstrated how subjects were 50 per cent better able to remember a list of words in a room scented with peppermint than those without.

herbal brain-boosters

There are many other aromas that have been shown to stimulate the brain in different ways. Two of the best smells to help you think clearly and optimize concentration are rosemary and basil. Basil is particularly good for counteracting mental fatigue. In the sixteenth century it was ground into a powder and used like snuff to clear the head; nowadays diffusing the essential oil is the most effective way to access the scent of basil for mental clarity. Add a few drops to water in the dish of an oil burner for an effect as refreshing as a brisk mountain walk. Alternatively, try crushing a few fresh leaves of basil, mint or oregano in your hand to release the pungent aroma.

Eucalyptus – both the fresh leaves and the essential oil – has a strong, cleansing scent that is usually associated with combating colds and 'flu due to its antibacterial, disinfectant properties. It can, however, also help to clear the head and stimulate the brain. The strong, herbaceous aroma of marjoram, meanwhile, can help to warm up the mind as well as the body. Sage, too, is a mental stimulant, but the oil needs to be handled with caution – it is safer to stick to the fresh or dried plant.

the sweet smells of creativity

Scents can also help to make you more creative. While it is the sharper, pungent leaf and herb smells that seem to increase mental alertness, frankincense, bergamot, rose and jasmine are among the most useful inspiring aromas. They are particularly good for freeing up the inventive part of the brain. Jasmine, for example, has been proven to boost creativity by 30 per cent. Similarly, a study at Cornell University in the United States found that in a test using word-association and sentence-completion tasks to measure creativity, the sweet smell of cinnamon buns significantly improved the subjects' performance.

Jasmine has been shown to boost creativity by

30%

choosing the fragrance that works for you

Because there are so many fragrances that aid mental effort, it is a good idea to experiment with the different categories – herbal, floral or citrus – to discover which one has the most positive effect on you. For my part, when my brain cells have shut down, I find that rose- and jasmine-scented incense sticks will switch them back on again. Nineteenth-century French novelist Gustave Flaubert apparently liked to work in a closed, quiet room with 'a familiar odour of amber rosaries and oriental tobacco'. Once you have found the scent that works for you, use it as an olfactory cue for focusing on the task in hand. You might become addicted to scented candles or essential oils but at least they are less hazardous to your health than caffeine or nicotine.

If you work from home, you could even try using a variety of different fragrances according to the time of day: a bracing early burst of lemon or peppermint to get you in the mood for work first thing; a whiff of rosemary or basil to maintain mental clarity mid-morning; and then maybe a refreshing spritz of grapefruit to beat the post-lunch energy slump. A recent survey by a British employment agency showed that nearly 30 per cent of office workers were against the idea of their employers pumping fragrance through the air conditioning, but many admitted that it was because they did not like the idea of their employer controlling everything. The beauty of the home office is that, instead of having a fixed menu forced upon you, you can choose the scent to suit your mood. If you need a confidence boost, for example, light a jasmine candle or joss stick; or simply inhale from the bottle of essential oil. If you are feeling a little sluggish, try diffusing essential oils of grapefruit, lime or lemon.

scented stationery

Various experiments by Dr Alan Hirsch in Chicago have shown that people will linger longer in a pleasant-smelling atmosphere. By the same principle, even your paperwork and the letters that you send could have a positive effect – by capturing the recipient's attention for longer.

In her book *The Fragrant Mind,* Valerie Ann Worwood suggests that to fragrance your stationery you should put it into a cardboard box, drop a few drops of essential oil into the box and then wrap it in a plastic bin bag, leaving it for at least 24 hours to allow the aroma to permeate the paper inside. For professional purposes Worwood advises avoiding overly feminine or floral fragrances and choosing coriander, lemon or bergamot instead, as they evoke confidence. Alternatively, you can place 5 to 10 drops of your favourite essential oil on a piece of cotton wool and leave it in the box where you keep your writing paper for at least two weeks. You might also like to try fragrancing your favourite books by spraying pieces of blotting paper with fragrance and placing that between the pages. You can even use a smell to make clients settle their accounts more quickly. It has been shown that, when sprayed on an invoice, an odour called Aeolus 7, which smells like sweat, induces tardy customers to pay up.

eliminating the negative

Many big offices are said to suffer from 'sick building' syndrome; all offices can be very toxic environments. The combination of computer emissions and volatile compounds from the photocopier and fax can produce a very unhealthy space. While you can do little to combat this, there are some steps that you can take to freshen the air. You could, like the New York Stock Exchange, introduce the Peruvian cactus *Cereus uruguayanus,* with its white, scented flowers, which apparently reduces the electromagnetic emissions from computers. Other species, such as the spider plant, while not scenting the air, will help to freshen it and reduce pollutants. Position such plants near your computer or fax.

You can also improve the ambience in your office by investing in an ionizer. This works by filling the air with negative ions. Negative ions are found in large numbers by the sea, on mountains and in coniferous forests, thus helping to explain why people feel so good in these environments. Similarly, negative ions will help to freshen the air in your study (just think how fresh the air is after an electrical storm) and enhance your mood. Fresh flowers, too, are a means of lifting the spirits and perfuming the air around your desk.

the mechanics
of fragrance

Candles are the easiest, most convenient and stylish way of fragrancing the home office – and the flickering flame also creates a calming ambience. Feng-shui expert Sarah Surety believes that burning a candle on your desk will help you to concentrate for long enough to get a job done; while legendary American style maven Diana Vreeland was known for always having perfumed Rigaud candles burning on her desk. Remember, though, that a naked flame is always a potential fire hazard.

Alternatively, you can use essential oils, whose fragrance is released most effectively when they are put in contact with heat. Oil burners require a night-light underneath, so again, if you have piles of paperwork and magazines in your study, you should be constantly aware of the fire risk and extinguish them when you leave the room. Incense sticks are a safer option because the naked flame is instantly extinguished and the fragrant sticks smoulder gently, as they release their aromatic smoke into the atmosphere. Electric diffusers, which vaporize neat essential oils, are the safest of all and, unlike candle-fuelled burners, they can be left unattended.

Another simple but effective option is to drop a little essential oil into a mug of warm water. Or dilute a few drops of your chosen oil in water in a plant spray.

perk up with peppermint

In Japan and the United States there have been numerous studies undertaken on the effect of the smell of peppermint. It is very refreshing; good for lifting a gloomy mood; and is a powerful stimulant (sometimes given to those suffering from shock), making it ideal for combating drowsiness. It also staves off the headaches that can be so debilitating if you have been poring over paperwork or staring at a screen for too long. Equally, given its antiseptic quality, it is a good essential oil to use in a room spray to combat colds and 'flu. Japanese car manufacturers are considering plans for a car that squirts peppermint from the steering wheel at frequent intervals to keep the driver awake. (Interestingly, when I was in Vietnam recently I noticed that the bus driver sniffed peppermint balm frequently in order to stop himself nodding off during the long 14-hour journey. Fortunately, it seemed to work!)

basil for clarity

Once used as an ingredient in an oil for anointing kings, basil is today one of the most popular herbs all over the world. Although today the plant grows wild all over the Mediterranean, it actually originated in Asia, and there are many different varieties. The delicious spicy-sweet smell of basil is an excellent antidote to mental fatigue, second only to rosemary in its clarifying effect on the brain. The essential oil has a yellowy colour and antiseptic properties. Its uplifting aroma is also said to drive away melancholy. If you are using the fresh herb, tear rather than cut the leaves to release the aroma.

coriander for concentration

The fresh, spicy smell of coriander can also be used to aid concentration and enhance memory. It is also believed to encourage assertiveness and confidence – useful before an important work telephone call or meeting. Beware however, since as well as stimulating the brain, coriander also has a stimulating effect on the appetite. The aroma of the essential oil is very similar to the smell of freshly crushed coriander seeds. The herb grows wild as well as being cultivated in the Far East, Spain and North Africa.

top tips for offices

• Vaporize lavender oil to calm your nerves on a particularly stressful day.

• Trying to remember a speech or presentation? Sprinkle different drops of essential oils on each of your cue cards to trigger your memory by scent association.

• Keep a bottle of basil oil on your desk. Sniff a few drops on a handkerchief to clear your brain before an important phone call.

• Add a few drops of grapefruit oil to a mug or bowl of warm water and keep it on your desk to combat lethargy.

• Burn a rose-scented candle or joss stick to promote a more positive atmosphere if you are in a negative mood.

• To repel bugs and bacteria, use a solution of tea tree oil or eucalyptus in water to wipe telephone receivers.

concentration potions

2 drops of bergamot
1 drop of basil
1 drop of coriander

2 drops of juniper
2 drops of lemon

2 drops of grapefruit
2 drops of bergamot
1 drop of eucalyptus

study
scents

5 bathe

the beauty of the bath

The bathroom is the best room in which to luxuriate in fragrance and enjoy the benefits of essential oils. It is the place to invigorate the body and wake up the senses at the start of the day, or to dissipate stress and recharge the mental batteries at its end. Interestingly, the ancient Greek verb 'to bathe' also means to drive sadness from the mind. Bathing can be deeply therapeutic. At the most basic level, submerging the body in warm water encourages relaxation, dissolving any knots of stress in the muscles and leaving the body feeling looser.

A bath without fragrance is like toast without butter. Whether it is a long half-hour soak or a quick five-minute dip, the cleansing process can be greatly enhanced by essential oils, detoxifying bath salts, scented candles or just plain, old-fashioned, perfumed bubble bath. With the right fragrance, bathing can be a deliciously sensual ritual. A languid soak in water laced with lavender essence is probably the very best way to beat insomnia; while a dip in refreshing grapefruit can really revitalize you. Bathing can be anything that you want it to be: relaxing, invigorating or sleep-inducing, depending on your mood and chosen fragrance.

Ever since people began to bathe, bathrooms have been more than just a means of getting clean. Roman baths were communal, lavishly decorated and a hub of social life, while the Greek physician Hippocrates noted the medicinal benefits of herbal and aromatic baths: 'A perfumed bath and a scented massage every day is the way to good health,' he claimed.

The earliest and simplest way to scent bath water was with a bundle of herbs or flowers tied in muslin but different cultures have developed different bathing methods. In Japan you cleanse yourself outside the bath and only get into the tub after you have washed. On 5 May – to celebrate boy's day – iris leaves are added to a child's bath, and fashion designer Issey Miyake recalls: 'We used to put thick pieces of orange peel in the water and its perfume used to mingle with that of the bathtub.' While bath water in Bali is scattered with petals of exotic blooms, scented candles tend to engage the senses of the Westerner.

the aromatherapy bath

The best way to enjoy the physical and mental benefits of essential oils is to add them to the bath. To prepare an aromatherapy bath, first fill the bathtub with warm water. Essential oils are highly volatile so wait until you are ready to step into the tub before diluting 6 to 8 drops of your chosen oil in 1 tablespoon of carrier vegetable oil and pouring it onto the surface of the water. Make sure the bathroom door is closed so that the fragrant vapours cannot escape. Then simply lie back and inhale deeply for at least ten minutes, allowing yourself to be cocooned in fragrance. The warmth of the water helps you to absorb the oil through the skin; inhaling the aromatic vapours allows its therapeutic effects to enter the bloodstream via the lungs.

Some essential oils, including basil, cinnamon, clove, peppermint, thyme and ginger, are skin irritants and should be used in very small doses in baths or not at all; many, also, should not be used during pregnancy or if you are taking any form of medication. The most popular oils for use in the bath are lavender, which encourages relaxation and sleep, and eases muscular tension; camomile, which induces sleep and soothes skin complaints; marjoram, which eases muscular pain; and rosemary, which has stimulating properties. Citrus oils such as grapefruit, lemon or bergamot are also popular for their invigorating and uplifting effects, but are best used in the morning.

a scented haven

The average bathroom contains all kinds of fragrant pleasures: bubble baths, body lotions, soaps and other potions. Ideally, you should avoid having too many different aromas within a confined space: a pungently fragranced soap can clash with scented bath water, and that will reduce the olfactory benefits. While some fragranced products do mix quite well – a lime-scented soap with a grapefruit shower gel, for example, or jasmine bath oils with a rose-scented candle – it is best to try to streamline your products so that the fragrances work in harmony.

Try also to keep the chemical cleansers you use in your bathroom to a minimum. Not only do they smell unpleasant and synthetic but many contain toxic ingredients. Instead, wipe surfaces with a damp cloth containing 2 or 3 drops of a citrus or pine essential oil, which will kill bacteria. Lemon, lime and green tea are refreshing scents suitable for keeping the bathroom smelling clean; a green-tea-fragranced candle is ideal for purifying the air.

Interior designer John Pawson believes that the bathroom of the future will have underfloor heating, a bathtub big enough for the whole family to soak in and a retractable roof so that you can bathe under the stars. Even if this sounds like 'another world' and your bathroom is so cramped that it can only just about accommodate one person, there are still steps that you can take to ensure that it is a sensory pleasure zone. Firstly, avoid carpets in the bathroom as they can become mouldy and smelly when damp and there is nothing worse than a clammy carpet underfoot. Instead, opt for a tiled floor or smooth wooden duckboards and use generous bathmats to soak up any excess water. Deep-pile rag rugs feel luscious underfoot and an occasional spritz with a solution containing a drop or two of essential oil will keep them smelling fragrant. Warm, fluffy towels, scented with the same oil that you have used in your bath will add to the sensual experience of bathing: simply dilute 5 drops of your chosen essential oil (grapefruit or lime in the morning; rose or jasmine at the end of the day) in a plant spray and spritz the towels – or freshen the air with it. Alternatively, if you spritz your towels with your favourite perfume and leave them on a radiator, that fragrance will permeate the air.

bathroom potpourri

The zingy rinds of lemon, lime or orange work well in an uplifting, get-up-and-go potpourri, while a simple bowl of dried lavender flowers will delicately scent your bathroom and help to create a calming atmosphere. You could also make a special potpourri for the bathroom using essential oils of rose geranium and lemongrass to purify the air and promote balance and a sense of wellbeing. Stylist Claire Richardson suggests filling a glass vase with a selection of white sand, sea-smoothed glass, pebbles, driftwood or shells, mixing in some dried lemon verbena and sprinkling with essential oils of rose geranium and lemongrass.

'A **perfumed** bath and a
scented massage every day
is the way to **good** health.'

Hippocrates

'Grapefruit is clean, **unfussy** and **modern**, like a Calvin Klein wardrobe. It is a staple for me, especially in the **room sprays** in my home-fragrance range.'

Jo Malone, perfumer

wake-up call

The bathtub is not just for winding down at the end of a stressful day. For the bleary-eyed and sleep-starved, who dread the moment when the alarm goes off, a bath or shower infused with zingy, uplifting citrus scents gives as much of a kickstart in the morning as a cup of strong, black coffee. Grapefruit is ideal for those who have over-indulged the night before as grapefruit oil added to bath water eliminates toxins very effectively and is particularly beneficial to the liver. Other fragrances guaranteed to revitalize the senses and get you going on a sluggish morning are mandarin, bergamot and lime, which all have fresh, energizing aromas. You can either use soaps or shower gels heavily loaded with these optimistic citrus scents; or vaporize the oils in the bathroom; or add 4–6 drops of grapefruit, bergamot or lemon to a bathtub of warm water. Another good wake-up blend comprises 3 drops of basil (to stimulate the brain) with 3 drops each of lemon, cypress, neroli and bergamot oils.

grapefruit *(citrus paradisii)*

Sharp, light and exhilarating, grapefruit is closely associated with cleanliness and is the antithesis of heavy-handed floral or musky smells. Grapefruit has only been cultivated commercially since the nineteenth century and so it is a relative newcomer to the fragrance industry's lexicon of ingredients. There are many different types of grapefruit tree but the best for essential oil come from Brazil, Florida or Israel. The fresh, citrus oil is expressed from the peel. Grapefruit's sunny, sparkling smell is good for lifting gloom and is said to have antidepressant qualities.

the sensual soak

Early femme fatale Cleopatra knew a thing or two about how to create a hedonistic bathtime experience; she bathed in milk laced with exotic aromatherapy oils, such as rose and myrrh. References to bathing as a prelude to amorous pursuits can be found throughout history. The Old Testament relates how Esther bathed in myrrh for six months before capturing the heart of the King of Persia. And in Roman times the bathhouse became a place of such extensive sybaritic activity that the Roman word for bath became synonymous with 'brothel'.

To create your own sensual bath experience, opt for luxurious oils such as jasmine or rose. Although these are two of the most expensive oils, their effect is very powerful. Along with ylang ylang, they can calm the nervous system and they are also said to have antidepressant qualities. To make bathing an even greater sensual experience, place fragrant candles around the edge of the bath or in clusters on the floor to create a soft, romantic light. You could also scatter fragrant rose petals in the bathtub.

G K Chesterton said, 'Man does not live by soap alone' – nor by just hot water. A perfunctory shower just cannot compete with the delicious pleasure of bathing, and it is worth investing a little time and effort in making bathtime more seductive to perfect the art of bathing beautifully.

love potion for women
8 drops of bergamot
5 drops of clary sage
4 drops of jasmine

love potion for men
7 drops of patchouli
4 drops of jasmine
4 drops of black pepper

sensual

'A bath surrounded by flickering candles and **scented** with a few drops of your favourite **essential** oil is one of the greatest – yet **most** affordable – luxuries in life.'

Noella Gabrielle, aromatherapist for Elemis

winter warmers

Spicy fragrances such as ginger, cinnamon, clove or black pepper are very stimulating and warming. So, on chilly winter mornings or evenings (many of the spicy oils are also aphrodisiacs) it is worth filling your bathroom with the smell of spice and all things nice, remembering that both cinnamon and clove oils are skin irritants and should not be used directly on the skin or in baths. To warm up physically and cheer yourself in miserable weather – a combined physical and mental glow – mix 3 drops of ginger essential oil with 2 drops of frankincense and 1 drop of patchouli.

Ginger is particularly good to use during the winter months – even a ginger-scented candle seems to repel winter blues. In Chinese medicine it is said to prevent chills and rheumatic conditions and is believed to be the perfect antidote to cold, damp weather as it enhances circulation. There are many ready-made bath oils that contain ginger, which smells particularly delicious when it is combined with nutmeg. (It was a nutmeg and ginger bath oil that launched the career of perfumer Jo Malone.) You can make your own warming ginger bath simply by grating a piece of fresh ginger into a muslin bag and hanging it from the tap so that the warm water runs over it as the bathtub fills.

Marjoram is another circulation booster that is ideal for winter baths. Its warm, peppery, slightly woody aroma is very comforting in cold weather. A hot bath containing 6 drops of marjoram essential oil will warm up both mind and body and can help to alleviate the unenviable misery of a cold.

zen scents

To promote Zen calmness and peace of mind at the end of a trying day, use 2–3 drops of frankincense oil in a relaxing bath. Frankincense is a sweet-smelling resin from Arabia which is used in treatment for stress and depression. Other fragrances known to relax, soothe and de-stress, and which can be added to the bath, include geranium, neroli (orange blossom), sandalwood, rose, jasmine, ylang ylang, lavender, camomile, rosewood and melissa.

mood-boosting baths

Geranium has strong antidepressant qualities, making it one of the most effective aromas if you need to drive away feelings of gloom or regulate unpredictable mood swings. It also has a balancing effect on skin – ideal for both very dry and very oily skins. If you find it too sweet, it blends well with many other oils, particularly lavender and bergamot.

Melissa, also known as lemon balm, is another 'happy' oil. Its uplifting citrus smell dispels negative emotions and soothes the mind. Use in a diluted form in the bath – put 3 or 4 drops in a carrier vegetable oil before adding it to the water – as too much can irritate the skin. It should not be used by pregnant women.

summer coolers

When the temperature rises, certain scents can be very cooling and refreshing: the best for this purpose are grapefruit, cucumber and mint. You should never use more than 3 drops of peppermint oil in a bath, since it can irritate sensitive skin – at best prompting a tingling sensation. However, there are many shower gels and bath products that contain its zingy aroma. If, though, you prefer the smell of cucumber, you could try the following tip from Crabtree & Evelyn's book *Fragrant Herbal*. Extract the juice from a cucumber and add it to a basin of warm water. Splash cupfuls over your body as you stand in the bath or shower. Cucumber has a cooling, astringent action, which will leave you feeling refreshed, or at least, as the saying goes, 'as cool as a cucumber'.

fresh

detoxifying soaks

Grapefruit and lemon are both detoxifying and refreshing. But for a truly cleansing, detoxifying bath, tie a bunch of lemon balm and eucalyptus under the tap and let the water run through it. Alternatively, you can create an aromatic and cleansing pine bath by making a muslin parcel from the fresh tips of pine branches and suspending that underneath running water.

The best detoxifying essential oil of all is juniper. A few drops in a bath will cleanse the body and encourage the elimination of toxins. Although the woody aroma of juniper is not very appealing, it works well with citrus oils, particularly grapefruit, to produce a very cleansing blend. Juniper has a diuretic action and helps to combat cystitis and urinary tract infections. Its purifying effect is also said to extend to the mind and can help to combat cellulite, accumulated toxins and water retention. Juniper should not be used, however, by pregnant women.

sauna detox

If you have access to a sauna, this will give you the ultimate cleansing and detoxifying experience. Mix 2 drops each of eucalyptus, tea tree and pine oil with 500 ml (17 fl oz) of water and then put this on the heat source as usual. Breathe deeply while you are in the sauna as the pungent vapours of these three oils, entering the body by inhalation, are particularly good for combating winter colds and 'flu.

soak

tips for the tub

• For a soothing, sleep-inducing bath, throw some camomile tea bags into the bath while the water is running. Leave them to steep for a while but remember to remove them before bathing. The fragrance is very relaxing (and cooling in summer), and camomile can help to soothe allergic skin conditions, too.

• Green tea – tea bags or loose leaves – has a refreshing smell; its antioxidant and anti-inflammatory properties are excellent for the skin.

• Rosemary sprigs added to warm water creates a fresh aroma that helps to fight fatigue, making a wonderfully cleansing and invigorating winter bath.

• An aromatic mustard bath (blended by herbalists Culpeper) brings the blood to the surface and creates warmth in the body. You will feel glowing and relaxed afterwards.

• For a really refreshing bath, add quarters of lemon, lime or orange to the bath water.

6 sleep

sweet dreams

Whether you are asleep or not, you will spend a large
proportion of your life in the bedroom, so the atmosphere
that you create there is very important. It should be as
tranquil and intimate as possible – a place set aside for
relaxation, restful sleep and romance. When you open the
door it should smell instantly appealing, filled with sensuous
and relaxing aromas that form a contrast to the rest of your
home. Use floral fragrances here, such as lavender,
camomile and neroli, to help to quieten the mind, restore
equilibrium, and coax the body into a state of relaxation.

A scented bedroom can also set the mood for seduction, as certain fragrances are known to have an aphrodisiac effect on the body. Perfumed candles are one of the best ways to create a romantic ambience. Whether you want to transform your bedroom into a romantic boudoir, however, or to slip quickly into sound and peaceful sleep, or just to tuck yourself up in bed with a good book and a bar of chocolate at the end of a stressful day, scent is the ultimate way to enhance time spent in your bedroom. It is as much as part of the cocooning process as soft pillows, crisp sheets and a comfortable mattress.

sleep talk

Three of the best essential oils for creating a restful, soporific mood are lavender, camomile and neroli. Other scents that calm, relax and aid sleep include clary sage, camomile, rose, frankincense and ylang ylang. If insomnia is a persistent problem, it is a good idea to switch essential oils every two weeks, since as the body grows accustomed to a particular oil, it gradually ceases to be effective.

Lavender is the most effective aroma of all for inducing sleep. One of the best-known cures for insomnia is simply to sprinkle a few drops of lavender oil onto your pillow. Alternatively, spritz your sheets with lavender water; slip a sachet of dried lavender into your pillowcase; or keep a bowl of lavender potpourri on the bedside table. On a summer evening sprinkle a few drops of lavender oil on your curtains to keep insects and bugs away, leaving the window open to let the fragrance waft into the room on the night breeze. In winter, place a sachet of dried lavender inside the cover of your hot-water bottle and it will gently fragrance your bed and infuse the room with a calming, soporific smell as well as lulling you into sleep.

the lavender workout

You could even try 'The Lavender Workout': a new concept, recently introduced by a few select London gyms and designed to de-stress and clear the mind rather than burn calories. For an at-home workout, diffuse a little lavender oil in a burner, lie on your bed and breathe deeply. Allow yourself to drift away, visualizing yourself in a tropical paradise. Continue to inhale deeply for 40 minutes – ideally to a soundtrack of water lapping on the seashore. It is as simple as that. The Lavender Workout is said to promote spiritual, mental and physical wellbeing and, although it does not burn calories, physical benefits can include lowering blood pressure, and a reduction in stress knots and the build-up of lactic acid which can cause back pain.

sleep potions

2 drops of camomile
2 drops of lavender
1 drop of clary sage

2 drops of frankincense
1 drop of patchouli
1 drop of vetiver
1 drop of sandalwood

1 drop of neroli
1 drop of rose otto
1 drop of ylang yang

the scents of seduction

Certain smells can press a pleasure button within the brain. When we smell a particular aroma, it transmits messages to the limbic system of the brain, where our basic desires are housed. Just as one aroma can stimulate appetite, another can arouse the erotogenic senses. Although men are said to fall in love through their eyes and women through their ears, recent research suggests that actually we do so through our noses. The Neurological Director of the Smell and Taste Treatment and Research Foundation in Chicago, neurologist and psychiatrist Dr Alan Hirsch, believes that smell is the initiating factor in sexual attraction; while subliminal odours have the power to alter hormone production and influence desire.

Scents that fall into the category known as erotogenics include sandalwood, jasmine, neroli and patchouli, although many people do not like the smell of the latter (perhaps because they associate it with hippie culture and the 1960s). These contain olfactory notes similar to human pheromones, chemical substances secreted in sweat that can – on a subliminal level – stimulate sexual desire in others. Sandalwood, for example, which has long been associated with earthy, sensuous pleasures, contains a substance related to the pheromone androsterone, produced by both men and women and often described as 'the raw fuel of libido'. Rose contains phenylethyl alcohol, related to phenylethylamine or PEA, a natural form of amphetamine produced by the body when sexually excited.

Generally, scents that are considered to be aphrodisiacs work in one of three ways. The first group of scents, described above, work by possibly affecting the hormones. The second group of aphrodisiac aromas, which includes neroli, rose, clary sage and ylang ylang, put people in the mood for love by soothing the anxieties and stresses that are known to kill sexual desire. Rose and neroli can also help to reduce inhibitions. Other aromas, such as black pepper, cinnamon, cardamom and certain spicy smells, have a stimulating effect, which can work as an aphrodisiac if you are suffering from fatigue.

food aromas and sexual appetite

Dr Alan Hirsch has studied the sexual responses of men and women to different scents. His research shows that certain food odours can increase sexual arousal in men and women. The smell that caused the greatest degree of arousal in men was a mixture of lavender and pumpkin pie, with the aroma of cinnamon buns a close second. Curiously, a combination of Liquorice Allsorts and cucumber was the smell that had the greatest effect on female arousal, although the winner in the male study – together with banana bread – also had an effect on women.

Nobody is suggesting that you place a pumpkin pie on your bedside table, but it is interesting to note that the spices used in pumpkin pie, such as cinnamon, nutmeg and ginger, are all well established in folklore and aromatherapy as sexual scents – and common ingredients in commercially available potpourris, candles and room fragrances. Although culinary smells are not usually associated with the bedroom, Dr Hirsch's research adds a whole new dimension to the phrase 'spicing up your love life'.

sexy potions

2 drops of mandarin
2 drops of juniper
1 drop of clary sage
1 drop of ylang ylang
1 drop of black pepper

5 drops of frankincense
3 drops of bergamot
3 drops of orange
3 drops of lemon
1 drop of ginger
1 drop of cinnamon

3 drops of rose
2 drops of jasmine
2 drops of lime
1 drop of cinnamon

from bedroom to boudoir

Scented surroundings have always played a powerful role in seduction. The Romans scattered rose petals on the marriage bed, while in India bridal beds are traditionally decorated with jasmine on wedding nights. You too can use fragrance to weave some magic in the bedroom. The heavier floral notes are best for creating a seductive ambience and three of the sexiest aromas are ylang ylang, rose and jasmine. The creamy, sweet smell of the vanilla pod has also been shown to have an aphrodisiac effect on men. (During the early twentieth century, psychoanalyst and sex researcher Havelock Ellis discovered that workers in a vanilla-processing plant were in a constant state of sexual arousal because of their exposure to the scent.) Neroli oil – which is extracted from the flowers of the bitter orange – is another reputed aphrodisiac. This characteristic stems from its ability to calm nerves and anxiety rather than it having a direct effect on the hormones and it is for this reason that orange blossom has traditionally been used in bridal bouquets. The bitter-sweet scent of neroli also blends with the floral oils such as rose or jasmine to set the scene for seduction.

You can fill your bedroom with these aromas by means of scented candles – good for creating romantic, moody lighting, too – joss sticks or oil burners. Alternatively, make a fresh potpourri consisting of 2 tablespoons of rose petals, enlivened with 2 drops of Moroccan rose oil and keep it in a pretty bowl on a bedside table. You can perfume your bed linen, too, which is a more subtle way to heighten the sensory pleasure and luxury of your bedroom. Perfumer Jo Malone, for example, likes her bed linen to be changed, ironed and scented three times a week. While many fragrance houses now make linen sprays, it is easy to concoct your own floral water or spray using essential oils. Add 20 drops of rose, jasmine, lavender or neroli oils (or a combination of any two or three) to 200 ml (7 fl oz) of water in a small plant spray and shake vigorously. Then use it to perfume either the air or your bed linen. You can always take your personalized spray with you if you are going away on business or pleasure to evoke the mood of your own bedroom in the hotel.

'The soft **fragrance** of a boudoir is not as weak a trap as one might think, and I do not know if one should pity or **congratulate** ... the man who has never trembled at the **flowers** his mistress wears at her bosom.'

Jean-Jacques Rousseau

love-potion potpourri

Create the ultimate aphrodisiac potpourri to fill your bedroom with an intoxicating, seductive scent. Mix some pretty pink or red fragrant rose petals with a handful of vanilla pods and sprinkle the combination with a few drops of heady frankincense and sandalwood essential oils. Either place the potpourri in a bowl on your bedside table or use it to fill a sachet and slip it inside your pillowcase to enhance both your dreams and love life.

bride's potpourri

Courtesy of the herbalists Culpeper, this bride's potpourri recipe actually comes from an old cookery book. Mix equal parts of red rosebuds (for love) and southernwood (a love potion) with a pinch each of dried, rubbed rosemary and bay leaves. You can either display this potpourri in a dish in the bedroom or, for the perfect romantic gesture, make up heart-shaped muslin sachets to fill with the fragrant mixture. These can be hung in cupboards or wardrobes, or placed in drawers or the bride's trousseau to delicately scent clothes and bed linen.

the sweet scents
of the bedroom

all that jasmine *(Jasmineum officinale* and *Jasmineum grandiflorum)*

Jasmine, with its sweet, slightly narcotic perfume, is said to be 'the king of fragrance' to the rose's 'queen'. Like rose, jasmine oil is very costly, primarily because large amounts of flowers are required to produce even a small amount of oil. The best jasmine comes from Grasse, although good-quality oil is also produced in India and Egypt. The white flowers are gathered at night because the scent is more intense after dark; the oil extracted from them is dark in colour and very viscous. As an aphrodisiac jasmine works on both a mental level, dealing with anxiety and depression and promoting relaxation, and also on a physical level, affecting hormone production. As well as using candles, incense sticks and essential oil blends which contain the fragrance, you could try planting a jasmine plant in a window box outside your bedroom window, so that you can enjoy its exotic night-time fragrance.

'Does someone who has never experienced the **magic** of a field of **jasmine** or **roses** at the break of dawn really know what perfume is?'

Jean-Paul Guerlain, perfumer

Herbalists Culpeper have a simple recipe for making pink rose-water: Fill a saucepan with the red petals of any heavily scented roses, add water and bring the contents to the boil. Allow to cool with the cover still in place, and when cold, strain. Use this rose-water for ironing or in a plant spray to spritz your towels and bed linen. If you simmer a small quantity with a spoonful or two of sugar, the fragrance will permeate the whole house.

coming up roses *(Rosa centifolia* and *Rosa damascena)*

Rose has long been associated with feminine qualities and, as well as being the symbol of love, is known as the 'queen of fragrance'. Cleopatra filled her bedroom knee-deep in rose petals to lure Mark Anthony, for it was believed that when they were crushed underfoot, the oils they released would have a overwhelming aphrodisiac effect. While young girls were advised in the past never to inhale the perfume of tuberose in the evening because it was believed to induce a state of intoxication, brides in the harem bathed in rose-water. The smell of rose is said both to aid conception and increase the production of semen. On an emotional level, rose is an antidepressant and is said to boost sexual confidence in women.

The first rose oil was distilled in tenth-century Persia by an Arab physician called Avicenna. Established then as one of their best-loved fragrances, rose-water has maintained a long and strong association with the Arab countries ever since. Intensely fragrant rose oil comes from the *Rosa damascena* (called rose otto), which is grown in Bulgaria. Oil extracted from the *Rosa centifolia*, grown around Grasse in France, is called rose absolute and is said to have the most powerful sedative and aphrodisiac effect. *Rosa centifolia* is grown in North Africa, but the oil from this is slightly spicier, and known as rose maroc. Rose oil, which has an extremely complex chemistry, is one of the most costly oils to produce because it requires vast quantities of rose petals. A small amount of the reddish brown oil, however, goes a long way. Use it in your bedroom as an ingredient in potpourri or in dried flower sachets; burn a rose-scented candle or vaporize it in an essential oil blend.

Rose was mentioned in the *Karma Sutra* and the *Perfumed Garden* and is one of the most universally appealing fragrances. It is very versatile, so if it is too feminine for your tastes, you can mix it with other oils to give it an edge. It blends well with other florals such as lavender and jasmine; with citrus scents such as lemon or bergamot; and with masculine, woody aromas which act as a counterpoint to its sweetness – sandalwood, for example. For a captivating rather than cloying love potion, mix 5 drops of rose oil with 3 drops each of bergamot and jasmine, and 2 drops each of coriander and sandalwood.

love that lavender *(Lavandula officinalis)*

Lavender, with its sweet-sharp scent, is the most popular and versatile of fragrances. It has been used fresh, dried and as an essential oil for thousands of years. It has balancing, soothing and calming properties; it promotes relaxation, and yet, in certain circumstances, it can have a stimulating effect. On a more practical note, lavender has antiseptic qualities and also repels insects and moths. With silvery leaves and pale blue and purple flowers, lavender has a very complex chemical structure. Native to the coasts of the Mediterranean, its 28 species grow happily all over Europe. *Lavandula officinalis*, the delicately scented variety used in lavender water, is the most widely used.

ylang ylang *(Cananga odorata)*

The sweet perfume of ylang ylang, which means 'flower of flowers', is believed to be an aphrodisiac because of its calming effect, making it ideal for use in the bedroom. Eastern women use it to perfume their hair as a prelude to amorous encounters. Like rose and jasmine, it is very heady but it is significantly less expensive. The essential oil comes from a small tropical tree grown in the Philippines and Madagascar; there are lilac-, pink- and yellow-flowered varieties. It varies in shade from colourless to pale yellow, the best coming from the yellow bloom, picked early in the morning. Ylang ylang blends well with citrusy smells, such as lemon or bergamot, which act as counterpoints to its sweetness. It is best to vaporize it in your bedroom in a blend of oils or to burn a candle containing ylang ylang.

the perfumed wardrobe

In the early nineteenth century people used to fragrance their gloves, linen, slippers and fans. It is said that the Empress Josephine's wardrobe was so strongly suffused with fragrance that the scent of animal musks wafted through her apartments long after her departure from Malmaison. You can introduce fragrance into your bedroom, too, by perfuming your wardrobe or lingerie drawer.

For sensuously fragranced underwear, sprinkle a few drops of the essential oil of ylang ylang, frankincense or neroli onto a cotton-wool ball or decorative piece of wood and place it in your lingerie draw (being careful not to let it come into contact with delicate fabric). To deodorize shoes – particularly trainers – tuck a sachet filled with dried mint inside each one. Scented pomanders, too, are ideal for perfuming the wardrobe and for keeping linen cupboards fresh and free from moths.

how to make a rose pomander

Sprinkle about 20 drops of your favourite floral essential oil (such as rosewood, neroli, geranium or lavender) onto a small, dry florist's foam ball, distributing the drops evenly over the surface. Then seal the foam ball in an airtight bag or plastic box and leave it for at least 24 hours to allow the scent to infuse. Make a loop out of a length of pretty velvet, satin or organdie ribbon and secure it to the top of the ball with a hooked, S-shaped piece of florist's wire. Finally, cover the entire surface of the ball with scented dried pink or red rosebuds, using their stems to anchor them securely into the foam. Keep the fragrance fresh and strong by sprinkling the rosebuds with a few drops of essential oil as necessary.

'Fragrance is a natural
extension of clothing.
It can instantly make a
sweater into an old friend.'

Patrick Gottelier, fashion designer of Artwork

scents that repel ...

Moths and insects, that is. Try to avoid introducing chemical cocktails of any kind into your bedroom – there is no need to use pungent mothballs or chemical deterrents to keep irritating moths and insects at bay when there are plenty of natural scents that are equally effective. Lavender, for example, has been used for many centuries to protect clothes and household linens from moths. Simply tuck lavender bags – or bars of soap fragranced with lavender (or geranium) – between vulnerable sweaters in the pile.

Aromatherapist Robert Tisserand suggests perfuming a handkerchief with 6 drops of lavender essential oil and placing it in the tumble dryer when you are drying clothes. If you do not wish to scent your clothes directly, use lavender-scented drawer liners or wipe around the inside of the drawer or wardrobe using several drops of lavender or cedarwood oil diluted in 200 ml (7 fl oz) of water, to act as a deterrent.

When you are storing clothes long term, sprinkle a few drops of citronella, lavender, lemon or clove essential oil on a piece of cotton wool and keep it in the bottom of the garment bag or chest. Alternatively, cedarwood chips make a good moth and insect repellent. Fashion label Artwork provides lavender or cedarwood sachets with its handmade sweaters. It certainly pays to keep clothes smelling sweet as moths have expensive tastes and love nothing better than cashmere or silk.

'Our sweaters are designed to last for 10–15 years, which is why we provide scented sachets to protect them from moths.'

Patrick Gottelier, fashion designer of Artwork

UK

Aromatherapy Associates
Head office: 68 Maltings Place
Bagleys Lane
London SW6 2BY
Tel 020 7371 9878

Often described as 'the Rolls Royce of aromatherapy' in the UK, Aromatherapy Associates makes products of the highest quality – everything from fragrant burning essences and lamp rings to silk sachets of organic flowers for tucking into bed linen or underwear drawers. There are also fantastic bath and shower oils to fill your bathroom with wonderful aromatherapy aromas.

Products to note:
Deep Relaxing Bath & Shower Oil. The most popular product of all, this is a rich, heavy sensual blend of vetiver, patchouli and camomile – ideal for people who have difficulty sleeping.
Stimulating Bath & Shower Oil – this invigorating blend will fill your bathroom with the wonderful aromas of detoxifying juniper berry, rosemary and grapefruit.
Inhalation Essence – a blend of eucalyptus and peppermint, which helps to clear the head and fight germs when diffused in a burner.

Aromatique
154 Brompton Road
London SW3 1HX
Tel 020 7351 1950

Aromatique's decorative and divine-smelling products are used in some of the most famous homes in the world – including the White House and the Royal Palace of Monaco. Founded in 1982 and now sold in over 40 countries this top American range includes freeze-dried roses, room sprays, hand-poured candles and a bath line. The potpourri is intensely perfumed and capable of fragrancing an entire room. Seasonal fragrances include Spring, Summer Sorbet and Smell of Christmas.

Products to Note:
Scent of the Rose Room Spray, which smells as good as the real thing. This is the fragrance used at the highly fashionable Hôtel Costes in Paris.
Splendour in the Bath Décoratif – a divine-smelling potpourri.

L'Artisan Parfumeur
17 Cale Street
London SW3 3QR
Tel 020 7352 4196

A wide range of candles, burning oils and room sprays featuring sophisticated smells, designed to create an atmosphere. The most recent addition to the range is Thé et Pain d'Épices *(tea and gingerbread), designed to evoke childhood memories.*

Products to note:
Amber Ball – this evokes the smell of old books and libraries and is perfect for the home study.
Amber Candle – one of the most popular products for the home, this has a rich, warm smell.

Aveda Institute
28 Marylebone High Street
London W1M 3PF
Tel 020 7224 3157

The Aveda home range includes candles, sprays, diffuser oils and aroma rings in five natural plant-based perfumes such as Rainforest, Madagascar and Euphoric. Potpourri comes in three fragrances: Rose, Lavender or Spice.

Products to note:
Airmobile Kit – for freshening up the air in your car. Simply spray a fragrance onto a stylish green leaf mobile.
Plant Pure-Fume Candles. These hand-poured candles in distinctive Spanish green glass are available in five completely natural aromas.

Coty
For UK stockists call 01233 625 076
See also p. 142.

Crabtree & Evelyn
6 Kensington Church Street
London W8 4EP
Tel 020 7937 9335
For other shops and stockists contact head office:
55–7 South Edwardes Square
London W8 6HP
Tel 020 7603 1611

A wide variety of aromatic products for the home, ranging from traditional potpourris and scented candles (which are of excellent quality and seem to last forever) to the innovative 'Cooks' range, which includes food-inspired aroma sprays.

Products to note:
Vanilla Candle – one of the bestselling home fragrance products.
Cooks Potpourri – ideal for the kitchen, this contains cinnamon and slices of apple and orange to keep the air smelling sweet.
Patisserie Aroma Spray – this re-creates the warm, sweet smell of cakes baking. Spray it in the kitchen if you are trying to sell your house.

Culpeper
21 Bruton Street
London W1X 7DA
Tel 020 7629 4559
Head office: Hadstock Road
Linton
Cambridge CB1 6NJ
Tel 01223 891 196

The ideal place to buy ingredients to make your own potpourri. Culpeper stocks high-quality 100 per cent essential oils and dried ingredients as well as ready-made potpourris. The fragrant hot-water bottles, scented with rose or lavender sachets, are an excellent way to perfume the bedroom.

Product to note:
The Culpeper Cold Weather Bath Elixir – a foaming bath essence containing pure herbal essential oils of eucalyptus, rosemary and thyme. The aroma will fill your bathroom, clear the head and warm the body.

Czech & Speake
125 Fulham Road
London SW3 6RT
Tel 020 7225 3667

Initially founded in 1976 as a purveyor of bathroom fittings and accessories, Czech & Speake offers a range of six room fragrances designed to appeal to the discerning nose. These include Frankincense and Myrrh (a warming and exotic oriental aroma) and No 88 (very masculine in character). Rose and Mimosa are two of the more feminine, delicate scents. In addition to room sprays there are fragrant candles, vaporizing oils and burning sticks, which slowly release their aroma.

Products to note:
Rose Candle – loved by the Princess of Wales as well as Elton John.
Frankincense and Myrrh Room Spray – perfect if you dislike cloying, sweet smells and prefer something more mysterious – a favourite of Marie Helvin.

Floris
89 Jermyn Street
London SW1Y 6JH
Tel 020 7930 2885

Steeped in history, Floris's top-quality products have been favoured by royalty and fashionable London society since 1730. 'Floris At Home', a coordinated range of fragrance products for the home, was launched in 1999 and features top-quality candles (containing 10 per cent pure fragrance); linen sprays and environmental sprays. There are five wonderful scents to choose from – Seasonal Spice, Jasmine & Rose, Hyacinth & Bluebell, Aromatic Lavender and Oriental Bouquet.

Products to note:
Seasonal Spice Room Spray – a warm welcoming winter fragrance containing spicy orange, cloves and cinnamon blended with a hint of brandy. This is great for hallways.
Hyacinth & Bluebell Scented Candles – if you like the smell of hyacinth, you will love this spring-like scent. Use the small votive candles in the bathroom.
Jasmine & Rose Incense Sticks – these are ideal for creating a romantic but non-cloying ambience.

Jurlique
Apotheke 2020
296 Chiswick High Road
London W4 1PA
Tel 020 8995 2293

In addition to organic essential oils from Australia, Jurlique also offers specially blended mood-enhancing oils for vaporizing. These include Party Blend (which contains geranium, ylang ylang, orange and rose) to put your guests in a lively mood, Romance Blend (ylang ylang, orange and patchouli) and Clarity (lemon, orange, bergamot, pine and lavender).

Product to note:
Jurlique Bath Salts. These are infused with essential oils and double up as potpourri.

Jo Malone
150 Sloane Street
London SW1X 9BX
Tel 020 7730 2100
The most fashionable perfumer in London, Jo Malone started out by mixing her legendary Nutmeg and Ginger bath oil at her kitchen table and has since expanded her repertoire to include many perfumed products for the home. These include oversized bags of chunky potpourri, a variety of linen sprays and divine-smelling scented candles which match many of her colognes. Most innovative of all are the living colognes, which are designed to sit equally well on the skin as they do in the living space.
Products to note:
Lime Blossom Candle – the nicest smelling candle in the Malone range. It is so loaded with scent that it perfumes the room even when it is not lit.
Living Cologne in White Hyacinths – a clean, fresh smell that is so good you will want to use it on your skin.
Lime, Basil and Mandarin Shower Gel – not strictly a home fragrance product, but Jo Malone's bestselling product will suffuse the bathroom with a refreshingly clean, zesty smell.
Aqua di Limone Linen Spray – a sparkling, citrus scent.

L'Occitane
67 King's Road
London SW3 4NT
Tel 020 7823 4555
Head office: 237 Regent Street
London W1R 8PS
Tel 020 7290 1426
For mail order and other stores and stockists, call 020 7290 1421
An elegant range of home perfume sprays which come in chic glass flaçons like perfume bottles. There are many delicious and unusual fragrances to choose from – such as Apricot and Grapefruit (a fresh citrus scent), Melissa Pear, Tomato and Blackcurrant or Orange Nutmeg – all inspired by the fruits, flowers, herbs and spices of the markets of Provence. Scented candles, stylishly packaged in tins, and incense sticks and cones are also available.

Natural Products
For stockists contact head office:
2 Kimberley Road
London NW6 7SG
Tel 020 7372 4101
'We Live Like This' is a great looking range of bathroom products packaged in medicinal-style jars with bar codes. There are also stylishly packaged incense sticks 'for modern day hedonists' in a range of contemporary fragrances such as Cantaloupe, Frankincense and Myrrh, Spearmint, Moss and Strangefruit. Michael Sweeney who created 'We Live Like This' also makes own-label fragrance ranges for top stores.

Origins
51 King's Road
London SW3 4ND
Tel 020 7730 6116
Many of the fragrances in the Origins range smell good enough to eat. Bath products such as Ginger Float, Fretnot and Gloomaway claim to do more than make your bathroom smell delicious, by acting as 'a shrink in a bottle'. The Origins 'Sensory Therapy Inhalations' range of blended oils designed to be diffused in a burner includes Open Mind (for mental clarity) and Slumber Party (which aids sleep). The 'Clean Sheets' collection for the home includes scented candles, room freshener sprays and a linen wash. The blend of peppermint and grapefruit has the same effect on a stale room as opening the windows.

Penhaligon's
18 Beauchamp Place
London SW3 1NQ
Tel 020 7584 4008
For other shops and stockists, call 0800 716 108
A traditional English perfumer founded in 1870, Penhaligon's specializes in old-fashioned floral fragrances, such as Elizabethan Rose, Bluebell and English Fern. The home range includes lamp oils, room sprays and candles – which are of unbeatable quality and are packed with enough scent to perfume an entire room. Fans include Jilly Cooper, Donatella Versace and Lady Virginia White.

Product to note:
Lily-of-the-Valley Candle – the ultimate in good taste, this divine-smelling product comes as a set of three in stylish silver pots. A favourite of style cognoscenti, it is also Penhaligon's bestselling home fragrance.

Perfumes Isabell
For UK stockists call 01932 254 854
See also p. 142.

Price's Candles
110 York Road
London SW11 3RD
Tel 020 7228 3345
The UK's leading candle manufacturer, Price's was established in 1830 by two merchant partners. Florence Nightingale is said to have tiptoed among the Crimean casualties by the light of a Price's candle. The company now offers a wide range of scented and aromatherapy candles including special Christmas and Easter candles and tinned travel candles.
Product to note:
Euphoric Candle – an invigorating, citrus smell which is ideal for the study.

Space NK
127–31 Westbourne Grove
London W2 4UP
Tel 020 7727 8002
For other shops and stockists, call 020 7299 4999
Stocks a great range of home fragrance products ranging from Diptyque and other designer candles to its own brand, Space.NK.Home. This includes delicately perfumed candles, incense sticks and a linen spray. Fragrances include IV, Scenery of Spring – a white flower scent redolent of walking into a florist's store on a bright spring morning – and VII, Mediterranean Evening – a fresh, green fig-leaf fragrance. The pristine linen spray is a mix of lavender, apple blossom and violet.

FRANCE

L'Artisan Parfumeur
24 boulevard Raspail
75007 Paris
Tel (33) 1 42 22 23 32

This small boutique, opulently decorated in emerald and black, offers a unique and ever-changing range of perfumed objects for the home such as the Boule d'Ambre (amber ball). There are also room sprays, candles and drawer sachets inspired by the natural aromas of flowers, fruits, spices and woods. The most popular home fragrance is Mûre et Musc – an avant-garde combination of freshness and warmth. See also pp. 140 and 141.

Cir
22 rue Saint-Sulpice
75006 Paris
Tel (33) 1 44 26 46 50
In addition to stocking Rigaud's famous candles, this boutique offers some delightful incenses.

Dyptique
34 boulevard Saint-Germain
75005 Paris
Tel (33) 1 43 26 45 27
In 1961 English painter Desmond Knox-Leet opened a boutique in Paris offering the first 'Made in England' potpourris and pomanders and perfumed candles. The candles now come in over 30 different fragrances. The Paris boutique – which is always packed with models and style cognoscenti – also stocks the matching room sprays. The Fig fragrance – a warm voluptuous scent – is especially fashionable.

Annick Goutal
14 rue de Castiglione
75001 Paris
Tel (33) 1 42 60 52 82
This enchanting jewel-box of a shop stocks scented candles and other beautifully packaged home products to match the cult fragrances. Look out for tins of pebbles perfumed with Eau d'Hadrien – a symphony of Sicilian lemon, mandarin and cypress and the most successful of all the scents – which can only be bought here.

Parfums Rigaud
Head office:
9 rue Saint-Florentin
75008 Paris
Tel (33) 1 42 60 11 14

Rigaud candles are entirely handmade and are among the best in the world. Although Parfums Rigaud dates back to the early nineteenth century, the Rigaud candle was only born in 1950, and was created by Madame Rigaud whose idea it was to open a house gift shop offering environmental fragrance. The soft wax, which allows an optimum diffusion of the fragrance and uniform burning of the candle, has been specially patented.

Products to note:
The best known of the Rigaud candles is the first created, *Cyprès* – green in colour with a natural woody fragrance. Others to note include *Tournesol* (yellow with a tangy floral and fruity scent) and *Santifolia* (pink with a delicate rose scent). Fans of Rigaud's environmental fragrances include the Prince of Wales and Liz Taylor.

Le Saponifere
59 rue Bonaparte
75006 Paris
Tel (33) 1 46 33 98 43
A pretty shop specializing in products and accessories for the bathroom. It offers a selection of potpourris, silk sachets perfumed with vanilla, gardenia or cedar room sprays and decorative bunches of dried flowers, which are specially treated to release perfume over a long period.

ITALY

Profumo Farmaceutica di Santa Maria Novella
Via dela Scala, 16
50123 Florence
Tel (39) 55 216 276
Tucked off the beaten tourist track in Florence is one of the oldest pharmacies in the world. Established by the Dominican Fathers in about 1221, the pharmacy has beautiful domed frescoes, a marble floor and mahogany shelves. Glass display cabinets are full of old-style fragrances and all manner of essences. Among them are Pomegranate Bath Salts, Rose-Water, handkerchief extracts such as Heliotrope, and pungent, herbal potpourris gathered on the hillsides of Tuscany.

USA

L'Artisan Parfumeur
870 Madison Avenue
New York
NY 10021
Tel (1) 212 517 8665
See also pp. 140 and 141.

Aveda Lifestyle Store
509 Madison Avenue
New York
NY 10022
Tel (1) 212 832 2416
This store stocks the full range of environmental home and personal fragrancing products, all of which are based on the beauty of pure, natural essences. See also p. 140.

Banana Republic
552 Broadway
New York
NY 10012
Tel (1) 212 925 0308.
Banana Republic's new home range is a good source of all kinds of scented products for the home. The beautiful scented candles – called Beach House or Casablanca Lilies – are especially noteworthy.

Coty
Head office: 1325 6th Avenue
New York
NY 10019
Tel (1) 212 479 4300
The 'Healing Garden' range, which includes bath products, incense sticks, scented candles and sprays – all of which contain natural botanical extracts – is an integrated range for the home and body, based on the science of aromachology. There are four fragrance groups: Lavender Sensations (relaxing); Mandarin Sensations (energizing); Green Tea Sensations (balancing); and Jasmine Sensations (for sensuality).

Products to note:
High Energy Candle – an invigorating blend of mandarin, tea tree, ginger and balm mint.
Green Tea Incense Sticks – these have a clean, refreshing smell which is especially great for the bathroom.

Demeter Fragrances
Head office: 27 West 24th Street
New York
NY 10010
Tel (1) 212 414 4151
This cutting-edge company – whose name is taken from the Greek goddess of agriculture – broke the mould in home fragrance with unusual scents such as Tomato, Dirt, Leather, Cappuccino and Cinnamon Toast. 'Some of the most beautiful fragrances in the world are like a ballgown, but sometimes you only need to wear a comfortable pair of jeans,' is how Demeter's perfumer-in-chief Christopher Brosius explains their philosophy. There are over 80 fragrances in total. Celebrity fans include Courtney Cox, Sharon Stone, Kate Moss, Stella McCartney, Clint Eastwood and Cher.

Products to note:
Sugar Cookie Pick-Me-Up Cologne Spray – a warm baking smell.
Gin and Tonic Pick-Me-Up Cologne Spray – a zingy, citrusy smell that claims to lift your mood just like the real thing.

Floris of London
703 Madison Avenue
New York
NY 10021
Tel (1) 212 935 9100
See also p. 140.

Fresh
57 Spring Street
New York
NY 10013
Tel (1) 212 925 0099
Also: 1061 Madison Avenue
New York
NY 10028
Tel (1) 212 396 0344
Fresh sells quirky home fragrance products including Chocolate-scented incense sticks and Orange Chocolate candles. Everything is imaginatively packaged – soap, for example, comes wrapped up and tied with delicate wires and decorated with tiny stones. Fresh also stocks the beautiful French home fragrance line 'Éditions Esteban'. Fans include Julia Roberts, who likes the Linden & Wisteria candle; Candice Bergen favours the amber incense and Lisa Kudrow uses the Sweet Pea candle.

L'Occitane
For mail order and stockists in the USA, call (1) 203 629 0885
See also p. 141.

Origins
402 West Broadway
New York
NY 10012
Tel (1) 212 219 9764
This downtown store is in an ultra-fashionable shopping area and is especially worth a visit as it stocks new products in advance of the UK and Europe. See also p. 141.

Perfumes Isabell
Head office: 30 West 26th Street
New York
NY 10010
Tel (1) 212 647 7500
Perfumes Isabell scented candles are the creation of top New York florist, party planner and 'mood manipulator' Robert Isabell. They are popular at parties of the rich and famous in New York and LA. Fans include Giorgio Armani, Madonna, Whitney Houston and Ian Schrager.

Products to note:
Isabell Flowering Lemon Kitchen Candle is great for removing food smells.
Shimmering Bath Lights – votive candles scented with paperwhites. These elegant candles turn bathing into a hedonistic experience.

Suggested Further Reading
Tisserand, Robert, *The Art of Aromatherapy*, Saffron Walden, C W Daniel Company Ltd, 1977
Davis, Patricia, *Aromatherapy an A–Z*, Saffron Walden, C W Daniel Company Ltd, 1995
Bremness, Lesley, *Crabtree & Evelyn Fragrant Herbal*, London, Quadrille, 1998
Barillé, Élisabeth and Laroze, Catherine, *The Book of Perfume*, Paris, Flammarion, 1995
Hirsch, Alan R, *Scentsational Sex, The Secret of Using Aroma For Arousal*, Shaftesbury, Element Books Ltd, 1998
Worwood, Valerie Ann, *The Fragrant Mind*, London, Doubleday, 1995
Lawless, Julia, *The Encyclopaedia of Essential Oils*, Shaftesbury, Element Books Ltd, 1992

Stylist's credits

The publisher would like to thank the following suppliers for their generous contributions to the photographic shoots:

p. 1 white beaker, jug and plate, all White and Gray
p. 6 patterned cushions, by Claudia Bryant; plain pink cushion, White and Gray
p. 31 bowls, Tony Boase
p. 33 leather and linen cushion, Mufti; fur throw, Ever Trading
p. 34 linen and velvet throw, Noel Hennessy
p. 39 oak incense block, Twelve
pp. 40–1 mesh lantern, White and Gray
pp. 53–4 buttoned scented bags and raw silk scented pocket pillows, White and Gray; slippers and suede cushion, General Trading Company
p. 57 silk bolster, by Claudia Bryant
p. 68 ceramics, Mint
p. 87 writing paper, Mufti
p. 88–9 incense burner, Designer's Guild
p. 90 throw (over back of chair), Mufti
p. 101 soap dish and ceramic vase, General Trading Company; scented soap flakes in glass jar, Space
pp. 106–7 silver pot candles, Penhaligon's
p. 119 suede booklet, Designer's Guild
p. 120 bed linen, Volga linen at Cube
p. 121 fleece hot-water bottle, White and Gray
p. 122 glass diffuser, Verde
p. 125 ceramic oil burner, The Cross
p. 127 silk bed linen, Space; cushions, Claudia Bryant
p. 129 Moroccan tea glass candle, Cologne and Cotton
p. 131 incense stick holder, White and Gray
p. 136 silk underwear, Couverture; cedar eggs, The Holding Company
p. 137 linen heart, White and Gray
p. 138 soap, Cath Kidston; cashmere jumpers, Brora
p. 139 cedar hanger, The Holding Company; clothes, Couverture

Tony Boase
woodturner
Tel 01638 730 039

Bouchon
Catalogue 020 8749 7566

Brora
344 King's Road
London SW3 5UR
Tel 020 7736 9944

Claudia Bryant
Tel 020 7602 2852

Cologne and Cotton
Tel 01926 332 573

Couverture
310 King's Road
London SW3 5UH
Tel 020 7795 1200

The Cross
141 Portland Road
London W11 4LW
Tel 020 7727 6760

Cube
14 Holland Street
London W8 4LT
Tel 020 7938 2244

Designer's Guild
267 King's Road
London SW3 5EN
Tel 020 7351 5775

Ever Trading
Mail order 020 8878 4050

Floris
89 Jermyn Street
London SW1Y 6JH
Tel 020 7930 1402

General Trading Company
144 Sloane Street
London SW1X 9BL
Tel 020 7730 0411

Noel Hennessy
6 Cavendish Square
London W1M 9HA
Tel 020 7323 3360

The Holding Company
243 King's Road
London SW3 3EL
Tel 020 7352 1600

Cath Kidston
8 Clarendon Cross
London W11 4AP
Tel 020 7221 4000

Mint
70 Wigmore Street
London W1H 9DL
Tel 020 7224 4406

Mufti
789 Fulham Road
London SW6 5HA
Tel 020 7610 9123

Penhaligon's
16 Burlington Arcade
London W1V 9AB
Tel 020 7639 1416

Price's Candles
100 York Road
London SW11 3RD
Tel 020 7228 3345

Space
214 Westbourne Grove
London W11 2RH
Tel 020 7229 6533

Twelve
Mail order 0705 004 1458

Verde
75 Northcote Road
London SW11 6PJ
Tel 020 7924 4379

White and Gray
113c Northcote Road
London SW11 6PW
Tel 020 7787 8173

Quotation sources

pp. 33, 56, 128, 131. Barillé, Élisabeth and Laroze, Catherine, *The Book of Perfume*, Paris, Flammarion, 1995
p. 61. Grahame, Kenneth, *Wind in the Willows*, London, Methuen & Co., 1908
p. 65. Harris, Joanne, *Chocolat*, London, Doubleday, 1999

Locations

The publishers would like to thank the following for kindly providing locations for the photographic shoots:

Stella Blunt, Marion Cotterill, Kimberley Watson, Lara and John Mosley, Flat 2, 114 Highbury New Park, London N5 2DR and myhotel, 11–13 Bayley Street, Bedford Square, London WC1B 3HD. Tel 020 7667 6000

Author's acknowledgements

Thanks to the following for their contributions to *The Scented Home*: Polly Wreford for the beautiful photography; stylist Rose Hammick; art director Penny Stock; and editor Zia Mattocks for all their hard work. Thanks also to Robert Tisserand (for many of the aromatherapy recipes featured); Martin Holmes and Linda Harman at Quest International; Professor Monique Simmonds; Noella Gabrielle; Claire Richardson; Culpeper herbalists; and all the super-efficient beauty PRs, particularly Astrid Sutton Associates, Jenny Halpern Associates and Nina at Wizard.

Thanks are also due to my parents and friends for favours too numerous to mention, particularly Philippa Bender, Brigid Moss, Stephen Morrison, Tim Whitehouse, Richard Rawlinson, Debbie Lewis, Nathalia Marshall, Wendy Driver, Judy Douglas-Boyd, Noel Kingsley and E, my endlessly good-natured boyfriend.

A big thank you to Sarah Barclay and Carmel Allen for the introductions to the inestimable Ali Gunn and Venetia Penfold, respectively.